Messages from Mary

Points of Power

Points of Peace

Points of Prayer

Written by Sandra Lynn Sabo

Edited by Nisanda Albaugh

Magical Moments Press
P.O. Box 384
Gloucester, MA 01930

Acknowledgements

With Deepest Gratitude:

To my brother Mike Sabo whose unshakable belief in this book made it possible;

To My Other Half Art Riaf whose devoted support made it a reality;

To Nisanda Albaugh, my Editor since 1990, who has always had the patience to look at this book "one more time";

To Lise Ragan, Publisher Extraordinaire of Course Crafters, Inc. who had the vision for this edition and helped its creation all along the way;

To my incredibly patient Graphic Designers Frank Lucas and Laura Herrmann;

Thank you for making a dream come true!

Many thanks as well to my family:

To my Sisters who raised me and love me demonstrably;

And to all my Children: mine in birth, and mine in love;

For giving me the opportunity to live in the Love of the Mother.

Copyright © 1990 by Sandra Lynn Sabo

All rights reserved. No part of this book may be reproduced in any form or by any electronic or mechanical means, including information storage and retrieval systems, without permission in writing from the publisher, except by a reviewer who may quote brief passages in review.

Printed in the United States of America

First Edition Paperback 2004

ISBN: 0-9748576-0-2

Book Design by
Reunion Publishing Group

Table of Contents

Introduction	i
POINTS OF POWER	3
Attracting twin flames and soul mates	3
Melchior Speaks on Breaking Bad Habits	5
Confidence in Business	5
Praying for Relationships	6
Receiving Money	8
St. Francis of Assisi Speaks on Painful Relationships	9
Mary Speaks on Relationships	10
Karma	12
Relationship Problems	14
Grace	16
Financial Freedom	17
Loneliness	19
Spirit Guides	20
Christ Consciousness	24
Why am I here?	25
Crystals	27
Maintaining a Good Attitude	28
Going Through Changes	29
Sexual Preferences	30
Value of Gemstones and Money	32
Male/Female Energies (Twin Flames)	33
PMS	34
World Predictions	36
Archangel Chamuel on Love and Life	39
Personality Disorders	45
Archangel Raphael Speaks on Service to Life	47
Fallen Ministers	52
The Sacred Heart	54
POINTS OF PEACE	57
Auras	57
Help and Faith	60
Visionaries	62
Questions of Existence	63
Maintaining Attitude	64
Nature and Purpose of Emotions	65
Animal Kingdoms	66
Heart Problems	68
God's Covenant	69
Becoming Saints	70

Creating Peace	72
Dropping Your Ego	73
Holy Wars	77
Money and Love	77
Your Greatest Destiny	79
Welcoming Change	80
Meditation	81
Material Losses	83
Grace	84
Spiritual Experiences	85
Growth and the Simple Pleasures	86
Making Mistakes	87
Alcohol and Drugs	88
The Winds of Change	89
Balancing Your Karma	90
Sin and Karma	92
Mastering Emotion	93
Finding Your Spiritual Truths	95
Receiving Love through the Masters and Saints	97
POINTS OF PRAYER	**99**
Beauty and Grace	100
Praying from the Heart	102
Developing Faith	103
Getting to God Without Church	105
Mysteries of the World	106
De-programming	107
Giving Advice	109
Conquering Fear	111
Solving Life's Problems	114
Receiving Blessings	116
Putting Spiritual into Practice	117
Living Your Most Glorious Destiny	119
Learning Discrimination	121
Shedding Judgment	122
Being One With The Universe	124
Acquiring Virtues	126
Miracles Through the Glory of God	128
Manifesting	132
Laws of Creation	136
Your Spiritual Mission	137
United With God	138
My Connection to You	140

Introduction
Prayer to Safely Contact Spirit Guides:

"I ask to be surrounded in a sphere of Pure White Light. I invite my highest Guides, Masters, Angels, and Teachers to be with me at this time. I seek the answers to the questions, in my mind and in my heart. I seek a Blessing in every area of my life. Thank you."

These are the words that first brought Mother Mary to me. It was not my custom to pray to her, but shortly after saying the above prayer, she appeared to me: enormous, full of Grace. I suddenly felt well protected, nurtured, loved. Mary was the first spirit to appear to me without my direct invitation, she just appeared seconds after I said that prayer. She asked me to take a dictation, which I did. In the dictation, she said that she was the Mother of the Earth and that we had unfinished business together. I was to pray to her and to ask for her instructions and her help, and that in return, I was to help her as well. Thus began our relationship. From that day forward, my life has been intertwined with her energy. In the first years, she gave me instruction on how to pray, on what to pray for. Usually, I was to pray for some particular virtue for months at a time: "Pray for understanding," or "Pray for patience," or "Pray to know what is the right thing to say," "Pray to know what is the right thing to do."

It was after seven years of this relationship and several years of experience in doing written psychic readings, that I sought to undertake the writing of this book. Mary's advice to me has always been so practical and on the earthly level, and her spiritual advice, quite healing and protective. I asked her for readings that could be helpful to as many people as possible. The format was at her direction, short personal conversations addressing common problems and questions. Their order was also important to her, as she went from addressing physical and worldly issues in Points of Power; to improving one's relationship with self and others in Points of Peace; to speaking about one's spiritual path in Points of Prayer. In some instances she brought in other Spiritual Masters including Archangel Raphael, Archangel Chamuel, Beloved Saint Francis, and Beloved Melchior, to add their energy and insights. These mini-readings were done over the course of a year, squeezed between the time when I got out of work and when I picked up my daughter at school. The only changes to the original words were to make them readable as Mary tends to speak in sentences that run on, flowing-like-a-river-with-flowers-on-both-sides.

Many thanks to all those who helped me to bring these readings to print. The fact that you're reading this right now is a bit of a miracle for me. Thank you. I also want to thank my Teacher Nancy Risley who taught me the prayer to contact Spirit Guides, and all the Teachers that made these words possible. It is an honor for me to be able to bring this book to you. But more important than any other words that I can bring to you are these:

Mary, as Mother of the Earth, is available to ALL of God's children. If you want to, please do call on her yourself, especially in difficult times. Ask to RECEIVE her love for you, and ask to FEEL her love for you, as these things are really more important and fulfilling than any words she might have. With that, I give you her words, and hopefully her love as well.

Sandra Lynn Sabo 2004

Points of Power

❖

*A*ttracting twin flames and soul mates

QUESTION: Mary, what do I need to do to attract my twin flame?

ANSWER: Part of the problem in attracting your twin flame lies in the fact that you don't really believe that it is possible to be loved by another who would accept you as you are. This has taken years of training on your part to actually believe that you are unlovable. Beloved Child, how could anything be further from the truth? How can you have that which your heart longs for if you don't think that it is possible? Remember, experiences of the past are not the future. There is a difference here. When you walk through life with the impression that you cannot have something, you repel that which you want with your very strong beliefs. Affirmations would be helpful for you. It is time to change your thought patterns from negative and self belittling to a more positive tone. Find ways to love yourself every day. It is vital for you that you feel nourished with peace if you want to attract your twin flame. Think of ways in which you are wrapped with peace, blessed, graced. Dwell on your blessings until you truly feel them. Dwell on truly feeling blessed, for in this feeling is the experience of grace.

Let the heart be that which longs for this union more than the mind and the body. In the heart lies the strength to attract such a love. Before you fall asleep, ask to be united with your love in the sleep state. Ask for this often. Calm your mind and ask for the experience of feeling loved before falling asleep. MARY

QUESTION: I have been praying for my soul mate and am getting frustrated. What can I do?

ANSWER: Dear Child, we can see your frustration in this matter. To attract a love that is special to you, you must follow principles of self love. Pray to have grace enter your heart. This will attract more grace into your love life. Know that you would not be longing for this relationship unless it were possible. It is important for you to go through the feelings of longing. If not for the wanting, it would be difficult to appreciate a love so great. It is important for you to know the pain of wanting this relationship, for there will be times when you will doubt its significance. This is a good time for introspection; of finding peace within your heart; a time for not struggling with the self. A new partner would only mirror these inner struggles. Be intimate with the longings within your own heart. Your heart will, through its own wisdom, lead you to your love. Look not so much outside of yourself to find your true love. You must reach inward first, locate the depths of the love that you offer to this mate. If you were to find this person, what would you have to offer? Alone you must have peace, before you can have a peaceful relationship. Alone you must seek grace, before it is granted through relationship. Bless you, that you receive the grace that ever awaits you. MARY

Melchior Speaks on Breaking Bad Habits

QUESTION: I have been trying to break some bad habits for a long time now. Can you help me to give up those things that no longer serve me?

ANSWER: You would like to give them up? You ask to give them up?

Yes, I ask to give them up.

Then they will go, for you have asked to give them up. Continue to keep asking to give them up and go forward in a positive way. Understand though, it is important that you not place a deadline on that which you are asking to give up. For, if it were to take three months or three years to have these things never bother you again, would that cause despair? It may take some time for you to get to the point that you are so tired of having these things in your life that it is effortless to actually give them up. Continue to ask to give them up. Whenever you think of the habit, ask to give it up. It will go. MELCHIOR

Confidence in Business

QUESTION: I have been trying to start a business and when I go to sell myself, I fall flat. Can you help?

ANSWER: Dear One, this is a dilemma that you need to explore in greater depth, for you are seeing that your own belief in yourself is not as strong as it should be or could be. Do not your friends who talk to you about your business get excited at the concept? Do not some people endorse you wholeheartedly? This is a message to you, a blessing to your business. For, if others have the love and energy for the business and you do not, there is something wrong with your approach. The reason that you are falling flat is because you need to believe that you personally are worth the money that you are asking for your services. A great many people now think in the same way as you do, that they want to be of service. They place themselves so much in the service of giving to others that they cannot receive. It is admirable for you to want to be of service to humanity. However, I can guarantee you that in order to be of service to humanity, you also need to be able to receive support from humanity to continue in your business. Remember that you want to be of service, not of martyrdom. Work is an exchange in which you are as much a blessing to your clients as they are to you. Pray for clients that will be a blessing to you just as you will be a blessing to them. That eliminates wasting energies on other matters. Your struggle comes in when you start thinking that you are not worthy. Reexamine this thought pattern and, if possible, change right away. This no longer serves you. MARY

❖

Praying for Relationships

QUESTION: I have been praying for the perfect

relationship. I am 35 years old and beginning to feel the urgency of wanting love. Can you help?

ANSWER: Dear One, certainly you are feeling the pains of loneliness. We are asking you to examine certain policies and beliefs that were thrust at you in the beginning years of your life. You were not taught to be feminine or to surrender when you were a child. The militant parents that ruled your house taught you that the only way to have power was to have control. The only way to have control was to walk tall and carry a big stick. Now, as a grown woman, you are finding that this is not what you think a relationship should be. You are right. Indeed, the perfect relationship which you long for is closer than you think. We are asking for you to examine the feminine aspects of power. See the power in surrender and gentle love. Look about you for examples of grace. Look to those whose lives reflect surrender in a way that is empowering for them. Those who live in faith that they will be taken care of, have a great power indeed. This is not to say that I would want you to give up on life and expect that you will be taken care of. More, I want you to look at the grace that is available to you. You were your father's imaginary son and had to fulfill those male expectations. So the pressure was doubly weighty for you, as you had to be not only the little girl but also the little boy. Look back on your childhood and recognize the mixed messages you received regarding your gender, and see if you can't replace those messages with others more to your liking. Realize that within all men and within all women is a bit of male and a bit of female. In that way, you will be more receptive to being who you are always. Bless you, for indeed you deserve to be blessed.
MARY

*R*eceiving Money

QUESTION: I am not making enough money right now. Can you help?

ANSWER: Dear child, we have spoken of this before and shall again. I have said that in order for you to be able to receive more money, you must direct your mind and intentions towards receiving. All forms of gifts are eligible for this exercise: receive thank you's, receive smiles, receive hugs, and receive compliments. Breathe them in. Imagine that these gifts are actually entering your auric fields. The amount of money that you can receive is directly related to the amount of love that you can accept. Inhale love. All money, thank you's, smiles, and hugs are truly gifts of love.

Money is a form of energy, used to exchange love and appreciation from one person to another. Be open to receiving it. In order for you to receive, you must be vulnerable. In order for you to be vulnerable, you must surrender control. You can't be in control when you are receiving. And yet, you are afraid of letting go of control. Practice not having control until surrender is something that you are comfortable with. Allow yourself to receive daily. You will develop a balance between surrender and responsibility. Surrender to receiving love in all forms. Be responsible for your own thoughts and actions while receiving. You are not a victim in this matter.

Bless you, and do be aware of receiving blessings from me, for my blessings to you shall never end. MARY

St. Francis of Assisi Speaks on Painful Relationships

QUESTION: I have been in a very bad relationship for quite some time now and want to know what I should do about it.

ANSWER: Yes, indeed you would! The relationship you are in is really getting you to look at yourself, as a reflection, so to speak. Perhaps you can see that you are afraid of your own power through the fear in your partner's eyes? He reflects your fear back to you. You can also see, if you step back a bit, that you aren't really through struggling with this person. If you were through, you would be long gone. You cannot correct the errors of your own ways by trying to correct the errors of another. None of these things work, do they? If you would like to get out of a relationship or a situation which is causing you pain in your life, ask to learn the lessons of this situation so that you can move on. Once you learn the lessons, you are free to go about your business and make your life into what you would like it to be. There is nothing holding you to another except for your desire to be there. So, if this abuse is something that you attach to love, you will tend to stay. Logical? If love equals pain to you, you will stay in a painful relationship BECAUSE IT MEANS TO YOU THAT YOU ARE BEING LOVED.

Now, your adult mind comes to me and says, "Francis, how can this be so? I am in pain and nothing is really holding me here. I still can't leave." It MUST be that you are receiving some form of payoff in the process. People do not really want to make their bodies sick. But, they do. Why? Perhaps it was the only time in their childhood that they were shown love and compassion, when they were sick. So, if getting sick brings results that they want, they will continue to get sick for the results, for the payoff. Look to yourself for the payoff in this destructive relationship. There must be some way in which you derive love from this pain. Learn new ways to receive love and to love yourself. You are an adult now. You can make new decisions when you see the truth of your reality. Bless you, for indeed you deserve to be blessed. FRANCIS

Mary Speaks on Relationships

QUESTION: I seem to always have fights with my husband over stupid things. I want to have a good marriage but don't know what I can do.

ANSWER: Dear child, you say that you are having fights. Let us explore the dynamics of a fight. First of all, two people have to disagree over something. Usually disagreements involve policy over how things are to be done and what the priorities are. It is necessary for both parties to be interested in fighting for there to be a fight. There needs also to be some emotional energy to propel the fight. Otherwise, it would simply be a discussion. I understand your predicament and here are a few things that you can do:

1. Both of you need to agree that it is all right for each to have their own views. The reality of the situation is that you ARE both entitled to your views. You both had different backgrounds, upbringings and experiences. I am will-

ing to bet that what you now fight about is something that attracted you to each other in the first place. Over time and closeness, this attribute which is different from yours has lost its appeal. Your peace will begin when you both acknowledge that a difference of opinion does not necessarily need to be a fight; that differences are simply reminders to you to think about your own positions.

2. The emotional energy is the thrust behind the fight. If you could look at whatever your spouse is saying without the emotion, you would not be fighting. Anger comes from the belief that someone else is trying to take away your will. You hear something from your spouse that sounds like he is trying to take away your right to be or even your right to do, and the anger sets in. Look at the differences of opinion as just that: differences of beliefs. Your anger is there to protect your own will. You will do everything that you can to manifest your will; there is no need for anger. Much more will be resolved when you discuss without emotion.

3. Negotiate: If everything is not negotiable, the relationship is doomed. There are some things that you can agree on that you both think are non-negotiable, perhaps dating others while married, perhaps creating debt without consent of the other. But, other than these things that you will choose for yourself that are non-negotiable within the marriage, everything should be negotiable, or there is little hope for the relationship.

What fighting does is help you realize who you are in a rather tiresome way. Take the time to write down those things that you need to negotiate, and do this non-emotionally. Write down your feelings and impressions on these issues. Take the time to also write down the beliefs that you have about the issues. If you are fighting about money, write down all the things that you disagree on. Also, write down all the beliefs that you grew up with about money. If you were raised on the belief that a penny saved was a penny earned and he was raised that you had to have fun in order to enjoy money, you can see that you have a basic difference of beliefs and need to negotiate money issues. It helps couples to have differences of opinion for that is what provides checks and balances, much like your governmental system. You erode the basic relationship with the fights. Civility helps you to appreciate each other and love each other longer. Take the time to examine both parts in these fights and the consequences. If you don't want the consequences, stop fighting.

Bless you, you will find a way out of this, for you tire of fighting and struggling. MARY

*K*arma

QUESTION: Am I being punished for things that I did in the past? I have been told that I have to work off old karma before I can have good things happen to me.

ANSWER: Dear Child, there are better ways in which you can use this information than in carrying this belief. It appears that you are using the concept of karma as a punishment for yourself. Realize that karma is not meted out as punishment by God. It is something that people create for themselves and for others. If, for instance, you killed someone in the past, that does not mean that in this lifetime, they will kill you as punishment for your past crime. Indeed, this seldom happens. However, the karma, as it appears to me, is that you will be slowed in your process and in your livelihood until such a time as you find understanding, forgiveness, and grace connected to the past crime. Often the thing that you need to learn most is a lesson that you find yourself teaching to others. If you are in the position that you see others stealing and feel compelled to talk them out of this crime, often it is a crime that you are familiar with, you will find yourself lecturing about it so that you can also give this same lecture to yourself. That is part of the karma issue.

Now, if you had in the past let go of responsibility and let others be responsible for perhaps your children, you will in this life find yourself in the position that you need to take responsibility for others in a more burdensome way. This an example of karma as delayed learning. You delayed learning about being responsible for your children in the last lifetime, and in this life you will be presented greater responsibilities. Some would refer to this as karmic law, but I see it more as a delayed lesson. People can attach such heaviness to karma when they don't really need to. Simply go through your life doing those things that you know and feel are right for you to do, and allow the idea of karmic weight to go. Do not punish or condone yourself or even try to think up reasons why you are being punished or why you should be punished. It is not supportive. If you focus on punishment, it will come to you in greater doses than you want. Think of yourself as free from punishment and it will happen. Bless you, for I have helped you along on your path in the past and will continue to do so until you no longer need my help. You are, as are all men, women, children, and life forms, greatly loved by me. MARY

Relationship Problems

QUESTION: Why do I always seem to have problems with women that I am involved with? They all want to change me.

ANSWER: Dear Child, as you have found out, there is more to having a relationship than just showing up. One of the reasons that you have difficulty with women is due to past experiences with your mother. There are those things that, as a child, you resented about your mother. She was an authority whose approval would determine whether you lived or died. When you rest your survival on another, you tend to be very careful in your dealings with that person. So, if this powerful mother did something that you felt was unforgivable, you would never express it. Instead, as a child, you stored these resentments until you could release them. The perfect time to release them is with the next "mother" that came along. The next person that mothered you was a woman. The feeling of being mothered brought up in you the resentments that you had for your own mother. Understand? Anger and resentment have a very long shelf life and will store until you let go of them in some way. It does not pay to hold resentments.

You gave too much authority to your mother. You gave up the power in your life through surrendering your emotions to her. You believed that she could not make a mistake and that she could do no wrong, as any child would believe. It was important for you to believe those things while you were an infant because your livelihood depended upon her. As you grew older, you had the chance to learn and to know what it means to form your own decisions and opinions. Each time that you tried to express who you were, you were stifled by your mother. Therefore, you decided that it would be easier and best for your survival if you would conform to her wishes. This caused a new resentment as she did not accept you for who you were, constantly trying to make you into what she wanted. On the gut level, every human being alive desires the MOST be to loved for who they are. This is the basis to the commandments to love your brother, for indeed you would like so much to be loved yourself.

Now, in your older years and as an adult, you continually seek to be loved for who you are. And yet, you have the old resentments and the old patterns connected to your mother. You cannot help but feel that every woman is trying to change you, for indeed your experience of it is just that: women want to change you.

To break this pattern, you need to realize that your mother was simply a misguided woman, similar to the ones that you now date. Do they ever make mistakes? You bet. Do you think that it is possible that your mother made some mistakes with you, in raising you, in trying to make you think that she was infallible?

Certainly now, you can see that your decision to conform to her standards was your own choice. It was you who chose to change for whatever good reasons that you had at the time. Now you can decide differently, be who you are, and relax. These women don't really want to change you. They simply want to know who you are. Try to allow them to see who you are without having to put on the act that would impress anyone's mommy. If you really want another disapproving mommy, act just like you would for your mother. You'll attract another one. You don't need the approval of your mother anymore. Make decisions about who you are and follow through. Forgive your mother for her mistakes. Look for the blessing in having had such a mother. Look for the payoff in living through those mistakes, and they will vanish as issues in your life. Bless you, for indeed, who you really are is a greater gift to the world than the puppet that you have been. Be not afraid to be yourself, for you ARE lovable. MARY

Grace

QUESTION: Blessed Mother, what is grace?

ANSWER: Dear Child, grace is the softening and loving energy in all of your experiences. It is love granted to you for the purpose of easing spiritual growth pains. All healing, all accomplishments, and all forward movements are best eased along with total love. Growth can be painful, and it is grace which can ease this pain for you.

In the times approaching, men and women will more and more begin to try and heal themselves. In fact, a great many will be forced to. We are not speaking of physical healings totally, but core healings which involve the body, the mind, the emotions, and the spirit together. Many have begun the task consciously. Many fads will pass as the experimentation in self healing and spiritualism increases. Finally, after people's experiments begin to bring results and conclusions about their spiritual lives, men and women will begin to understand life as the integration of all aspects of their being: mental, emotional, spiritual, and physical. Children of the earth have a special challenge. Remember that I, too, labored these soils, and know well the sometimes delicate balance involved. Man is created from spiritual energy. This energy connects him to all other forms of life, those he can see and those he cannot. It is through this channel of spiritual energy that grace is passed back and forth from lifeform to lifeform.

Pray for grace to enter your life, your heart, your mind and your body. Allow for the gentle hand of grace to ease all growing pains. Life is a joy and a pleasure when you are totally healed. Bless you, for indeed, you deserve to be blessed with eternal grace. MARY

*F*inancial Freedom

QUESTION: Blessed Mother, I want so badly to win the lottery so that I don't have to work all the time. This has not happened yet. What can I do?

ANSWER: Dear Child, I am understanding of your desire to be financially free and independent. This is only natural, because inside of all men and women is the belief that they truly CAN be free. This is a core belief which is within the heart of every individual. Understand that what lies on top of this basic core belief that you are free and independent is a list of other beliefs that crowd it and make it hard to reach. Think of your financial freedom as something that lies at the bottom of a barrel. In order to reach this freedom, you must investigate what is lying on top of it and holding it down. You picked up some of these layers earlier in your life through messages that came to you from your parents and other significant adults. These beliefs link you to poverty. In addition, you have had your own life experiences to help formulate more beliefs which prevent your financial freedom.

You were told as a child that you had to work hard to get ahead in life. You choose to retain this belief as part of your experience. Exactly how does this belief support you? It reinforces at every turn that money is something that must be suffered for. So, you suffer to accumulate money. You will continue to do this until the day that you decide that this belief does not support you and you throw it in the trash where it truly belongs, not on top of your financial freedom.

You have additionally been told that if you aren't smart, you can't make it in the world. Well, there are degrees to being smart. Is it smart for you to continue to abuse yourself with this thought? Wherever you go, you will find people who are smarter than you are. And likewise, there will be many who are not as smart. The KEY here is to find and nourish and love your own personal gift. What do you do that makes you feel excited? What makes you smile, think, feel, love? THIS IS THE KEY TO YOUR SUCCESS: TO KNOW YOURSELF WELL ENOUGH TO BE ABLE TO APPRECIATE YOUR OWN GIFTS, WHATEVER THEY MIGHT BE. Make a list of those things that you love or do well. Ask others to help you with this if you cannot find your own gifts. It is the appreciation that comes from others which makes you realize that they don't have the same experience or gifts as you do. Stop comparing yourself to others in terms of success, and in terms of talents. You are graced in your own way. If you wish my assistance, please ask me to show you your gifts. I would be more than happy to do this for all of mankind. Bless you, for INDEED YOU ARE A BLESSING TO OTHERS. MARY

*L*oneliness

QUESTION: I feel very lonely and don't know how to deal with this feeling.

ANSWER: Beloved Child, there are many in the same predicament that you are. This loneliness that you speak of invades your stomach and heart with a heavy painful feeling. In these times, the soul is reaching out through you for solutions to age old problems. This is why you identify the feeling as one of being lonely, as if the mind thinks that there is something missing in the experience of being with one's self. Surely, if another human's company could have eased this pain, you wouldn't have this problem. It is inner loneliness that we speak of here. Many people are so split from their inner selves that they actually feel lonely whether others are around or not. When first born, an infant has very clear connections to spiritual, physical, emotional, and mental energies. Gradually, this infant is taught to experience life through physical senses. Often children are cut off from their emotions, thoughts, and desires by a well meaning parent. The parent teaches dependency on physical things, rather than self sufficiency. Men and women still feel the disconnection of this inner child who was shut off at an early age. You are waiting for permission to feel, to love, and to express yourself. You were taught to be what someone else wanted you to be. Now you can choose to be who you want to be: formulate, create, be yourself without censorship. Know that what you do is for the highest good, and give yourself permission to explore those things that you want to explore. With every decision, ask yourself, "Is this what I want?" Notice if your mother's or father's voice is making your decisions, or is it your own inner voice. To be FREE means to be self governing. Even a government that professes to be free needs to have self governing individuals. Govern yourself. You might as well steer your own car as to count on a dead relative to do it for you. Bless you, for I do have every faith that you will be free and work for your own highest good and the highest good of all. MARY

Spirit Guides

QUESTION: How do I know if I have spirit guides?

ANSWER: Dear One, you most certainly do have spirit guides. The simple fact that you need assistance now and again, brings your guides. Your spirit guides are around you because they love you, because you have shared a past life together, or even because their energy, or sense of humor is the same as yours. They are interested in providing for you a connection from their plane of living to yours. Understand that there are many more planes than just this one. Your guides may come from many places to be with you. Some of your guides will stay with you for the duration of your life. Usually they specialize in helping you in one particular aspect of your life. In the spirit world, we do much work, and we are each allowed to choose our work according to our love, our desires, and our particular need for practice in a certain area. Our work often involves the helping of other spirits whether they are incarnate in a physical body or not. There are some guides whose sole purpose is to bring a constant flow of love to you. For this reason, I do ask for you to be open to loving guides, that their love may promote your life to the fullest and greatest destiny. I bless you. That is, after all, my job. MARY

QUESTION: How do I know if I have negative spirits around me?

ANSWER: Dear Child, it takes a good deal of trying to attract that which you refer to as negative spirits. The most evil spirit that you now have around you is negative thinking. I cannot stress enough how much your society supports negativity. Have you ever told anyone good news, perhaps that you were happy, only to find that others really only wanted to hear bad news? This happens all too often. The mind sometimes gets trained to thrive on chaos and upset until it gets to the point that it cannot accept tranquility as the norm. Many people don't feel like they can be whole persons if they don't have a crisis on their hands. Why is this? Because their belief about themselves is that they are their problems. Perhaps their mothers told them as children that they were a problem. Whatever the reason, to feel that one is not bigger than one's problems is a serious mistake.

Why do you have problems? They are there to cause resistance in you. They elicit a response from you and help teach you lessons. If the lesson is not learned, the problem has a habit of coming back disguised in new clothing. Again and again, you attract the same treatment from the opposite sex. And you wonder why. Notice what this kind of treatment is trying to push you to see yourself. Others are simply a reflection of you. They are actors, mimicking your very life. Watch carefully, for these are your hints. Most of all, problems are there to push you into becoming bigger than them. Once you are bigger than a problem, it ceases to be a problem.

Focus on life, on love, on tranquility, and on God. There is a great deal of reward brought on by doing this. Allow peace and grace to rule your life. Where peace and grace rule, where love and life are attended to, no evil can grow. It is the law. Bless you, focus your mind, heart and emotions on those things that you want in your life, and they will come. MARY

QUESTION: I have been wanting to learn to be psychic. Can you help me with this? Is there anything that I need to know?

ANSWER: Dear Child, what you refer to as being psychic has many definitions. It is my feeling that you would like to get messages from your spirit guides, which is different from being psychic. This psychic or astral plane is composed of many energy forms. They often appear as through a fun house mirror. Your guides must pass through this realm in order to get to you. You pass through the astral plane in order to get to other planes of learning and existence. You do this regularly when you sleep. Because of the distortions in the astral realm, often it is not reliable to trust psychic information. Some of it is true, some of it is past, some of it thoughts for the future. You can develop a rapport with psychic energy, but you can't always count on it.

Try to develop an open communication with your own spirit guides. You will find this more rewarding. Your guides are around you all the time and are very interested in contacting you to bring you information that will make your life easier. One who pursues communication with the angels and beautiful masters that surround them is always rewarded with a greater understanding of their purpose. Dear Child, if you would agree with yourself that you can and will communicate with your guides, there is every chance that you will do this. There is a step-down place to the different realms known as meditation. Before you meditate, say a prayer for protection as well as to state your intention in contacting your guides. If you were to sit there in a state of meditation and expect communication without purpose, you would sit a long time with mixed results. Begin to meditate and invite your guides to be with you. They will come. Ask for assistance in answering a question. Your guides WANT to communicate with you. Write down one question that you want addressed and accept the first answer that flashes in your mind as one from your guides. This begins the communication: one question, the first answer, another question, the first answer. Over and over again, this opens the lines of communication. Ask for the feeling that they are with you. Ask for them to show you what their energy feels like. This energy leaves you with a supply of their love.

Remember that you have many guides, so you must ask for one at a time. If you ask a question and get many different answers, you must ask for one answer at a time. Often, in the excitement of their first contact with you, the guides want to speak all at once and you may hear many answers. You need to make the conditions for all the communications and be like the conductor of an orchestra. If you find that the guides are bringing you communications when you are not able to listen, you must tell them that a different time would be better. State the time, make the appointment with them, and stick to it. You will need to structure the communications and make the guidelines to suit your life and schedule. Be kind and gentle. Bless you, for indeed all of your searching will come to fruition, especially when you begin to have a relationship with your guides that is fun and helpful to both. MARY

Christ Consciousness

QUESTION: I have heard a lot about the new age and the coming of Christ consciousness. I try to do my best, but I can't see from where I am that I can achieve this Christ consciousness, that it is difficult to be a "saint" in this world where there are so many problems. Can you help me?

ANSWER: Dear Child, of course. It may appear to be overwhelming from where you are, I understand. Perhaps you will need to take a look at exactly what you are trying to accomplish. In order for you to achieve what is referred to as Christ Consciousness, you must first and foremost learn to accept yourself. You were born with layers of deceptive thought and mistaken beliefs. Whatever these are does not really matter now. What your challenge is at this time is to learn more and more about who you are and to accept yourself as perfect in design, intent, and love. If you can do that, mistaken beliefs will go and your life will be much easier. So many bemoan that they are not good enough, don't have enough money, don't know how. These are human time delays designed to hold back the inevitable victory.

   Your mind and ego struggle with the concept of your own divinity. Your mind does not like to take any journeys into the unknown. The mind is playing this intricate game with you, perpetually making you doubt your greatness. This is one of the reasons we suggest that you participate in daily mediations to still the mind and the ego. The mind would like to convince you that it has everything under control. Beware of one part of you convincing the rest that it is king.

To be complete, all parts must function in freedom. Be emotional when it is appropriate, be physical when it is appropriate, be mental when it is appropriate, all the while being fed and loved by the spiritual.

You appear to have certain expectations about your Christ Consciousness. Christ Consciousness is the discovery of, surrender to, responsibility for, and use of, your own inner power. Your life need not be modeled after the Christ. Simply it must be modeled after your dreams, your aspirations, and your love. You came here for many reasons and the greatest is learning. Every day there is much to be learned. Accept who you are, give and receive love with grace. Expect the very best of yourself. If you want to spend your time telling yourself that you are wrong, guilty, fat, ugly, not good enough in any way, forget it. There are far more important things to do with your life than that. Your world will change rapidly. Be accepting of change. Know that all change is accepted by a still and gentle mind. Allow for grace to move you now and always. You will find your way. MARY

❖

*W*hy am I here?

QUESTION: Why am I here? I didn't ask to be here.

ANSWER: Dear Child, it seems ironic that you stand there and ask me that question, for indeed, I helped you to come here and to have this life. It takes a great deal of wanting on your part to secure a place on this planet. There are just so many life forms that are allowed to incarnate onto earth.

Far more would like the opportunity and must wait. In order to understand the blessing, imagine yourself as outside of your body. In your present state of mind, you would not know where to go except perhaps to a school in which you could learn about yourself and your power and your grace in a better way. This is what earth is for, so that you can learn as much as you can about yourself and about your nature. Being in the physical body clarifies the issue of who you are as opposed to who others are. Because of this physical separation, you are able to see for yourself what your own beliefs and convictions are. Other people may come and go in your life. They may try with all their might to divert your attention. In the end, you are still left with yourself. That is one of the lessons of life, that you have to rely on yourself for decisions, actions, and beliefs. If you are listening to another who tells you what to do and how to live and think, you are copying, imitating, avoiding the task of self discovery. Do those things that bring you to the realization of who you are. Relationships help with this; work, love, career, sports, and politics do also. Your creativity is the source of your own power and self discovery. Do those things which involve your own creativity in life. Realize also that you asked to be here for the purpose of self discovery, for I was one of your sponsors. I come to you to tell you now that I DO have faith that you will accomplish this to your greatest satisfaction. This faith is firm and unchanging despite any changes that you go through, any feelings that you have. My faith lives in a consistent fashion to feed and support your mission. I sponsor, love, and support all of mankind. Each and every individual life is sacred to me. Bless you, for indeed I, your sponsor in this life, am always available to bless you. MARY

❖

*C*rystals

QUESTION: Do crystals have healing powers?

ANSWER: Dear child, many things have healing powers of one kind or another. All of life does have the power to heal itself and to help others heal. Crystals are a form of life which receive and transmit energy. They are used in receiving sound waves in radios and for timing your watches. Crystals pulsate with energy depending on their designated use. To answer the question, yes, they have attributes that can help energy to move in a consistent fashion, thus clearing away blocks that are energetic in nature. All of life is made of some form of energy, and this energy flows through your body. If some of the energy composing your body gets blocked, a crystal properly programmed to help the flow of this energy could relieve the blockage. The key is in proper programming. The crystal made for your watch would not be helpful for healing the body as it is programmed to run a watch. You can program your crystals to move energy that you want moved. As crystals deal in energy, you should program them in terms of energy. For example, if you want to feel better and happier, you could program the crystal that you wear to attract love and flow that love through your body. This is how a crystal can work to heal you. Crystals will receive your thoughts and flow in accordance with those thoughts. Programming of a crystal should be done with a calm and loving mind, mentally speaking to the crystal, stating your intentions. Many books are available on this subject. With practice and car-ing, you will accomplish your intentions. MARY

Maintaining a Good Attitude

QUESTION: Mother, how can I keep a good attitude when others around me have such negative attitudes?

ANSWER: Dear one, that is difficult at times, though I would like to help you. First of all, your attitude is the result of how you see your life and surroundings. If you see your life as one that is distressful, you will tend to have a distressed attitude. If you, on the other hand, look around yourself and see that your life is blessed, then your attitude will be one of gratitude. Remember always to look about and see that you do have certain advantages and blessings that others do not have. Take the time to see that others who have a negative attitude are not as blessed as those who have a good attitude. If you think that your attitude must match negativity for negativity with that of others, you are wrong. Your attitude should have the reflection of your own way of looking at things. If you were to look about yourself and say, "Why me? Why do I have these problems?" surely, you will find reasons to support this view of a problematic life. If, on the other hand, you were to look about yourself and say, "Why am I so blessed?" surely, you would find reasons that you are blessed.

Remember always to try and find reasons that you are lucky and blessed and graced, for you will then be igniting the principle of "Seek and ye shall find, Ask and it shall be given unto you." Every day, find the time to seek your blessings no matter what else is going on. If you lose your job, better to ask why you are so blessed to receive a vacation than why this awful thing happened to you. Attitude is a matter of perspective. Realize that no matter what else is going on, you are continually being blessed, regardless of whether or not you can feel it at the time. Bless you. You deserve to be blessed. MARY

*G*oing Through Changes

QUESTION: There have been many layoffs in my industry and I am afraid of being laid off. Is there anything that I can do to prevent this from happening to me?

ANSWER: Dear child, there are many changes taking place, both in the world and in your country. These changes are instituted so that those who are living on this planet will usher in what is referred to as the New Age. You will see changes on all fronts, political, economic, technological, and sociological. These changes will peak or make physical differences by the year 2000 AD. Many of the larger corporations will be made smaller, the highest will be made the lowest as was prophesied. As you are personally concerned for your own welfare, I will address that first.

The reason that you are in fear is that you think that something that you value, your means of survival, will be taken away. The mind fears change, for it is comfortable dealing with that which it ALREADY KNOWS. It has a difficult time believing anything that it has not yet experienced or seen or felt through one of the senses. Do you ever remember a time in your life when you were about to participate in something new and felt fear? After the experience, you wondered what you were ever afraid of. It is very common to be afraid of the unknown. There are some who thrive on exploring the unknown and the unexperienced, but they are few and far between. The majority of mankind continues to be stuck in their fearful minds. Perhaps you could change how you look at this situation. To the mind, this is an unknown and the mind doesn't like unknowns. You need not suffer such an emotional reaction if you were to deal with the mind separately.

The mind would be calmer if you had an alternative plan. If you took the time to realize the frailties of your own mind, the fear would lessen for you. When you are operating from a place of fear, less good will come from your actions. Fear can cloud the mind totally from even making a contingency plan. Often fear can freeze an individual from making any moves at all. In those situations, it takes courage to walk through the unknown. For, indeed, courage is the ability to act in the presence of fear. To answer your question, yes, there are two things that you can do: 1. Separate the emotion of fear from the thinking process. Tell the mind that it has gone through the unknown before and survived just fine and, 2. Make a contingency plan so that when the time comes for you to make a move, you can have the courage to do what is necessary.

You will see many changes, more than the one that you talk about. Some will affect your life and some won't. The more you can adjust to change and accept change, the better off you will be. Your life will not be boring. Bless you, for you will survive the changes quite well. MARY

Sexual Preferences

QUESTION: My daughter has just told me that she is

gay. I don't believe in this and don't approve. What can I do about it?

ANSWER: Dear child, there is nothing that you can do about her way of life now. Your job as a parent was to provide shelter and nourishment for her body, mind, and soul until such a time as she was ready to be independent. It is time for you to let go of this position, for she is now independent. Parenting is, on the one hand a full time job, but on the other, a temporary position. You have done everything you possibly could to love and support your children while they were in your home. You need to let go of them now that they have left. If you think that your child is making a mistake that cannot be corrected, there are two things that you can do to make yourself feel better. One is to say something to her, express yourself. Another is to simply realize that all of life is experiential and that even your daughter will learn something from everything that she does. There are no lost lessons, one does not go backwards. Console yourself in the fact that no matter what, she is learning.

Another reason that you are concerned is because you feel that it is a reflection of yourself when your child goes against what neighbors and relatives would consider "the norm." No matter what, she is your daughter, and you are perfectly in the right if you choose to love her, no matter what her decisions. Your loyalty to her requires courage on your part. But, I do assure you, it will be highly rewarding.

Additionally, just as she is learning, you too are learning something. Look at this experience for what you can learn about yourself that will help you to see yourself in a better light. What can you learn from this that would make it an absolute blessing to you? Bless you, for I do know that you will find the answer to that question. MARY

Value of Gemstones and Money

QUESTION: What are gems? Are they a sign of vanity?

ANSWER: Dear Child, for many years, gemstones have been of value to mankind. In many ways, the gemstones which are revered on this planet are reflections of man's soul. They express for men and women what they should feel about themselves inwardly. At times, you will find that it is those that might be considered vain who are concerned with wearing and owning gems. There is a reason for this. It is those who are vain and prideful that NEED the reminder of their personal value the most. It is those who inwardly know God's love and grace flow through them, that don't need the reminder. Understand, this in no way means that reminders of one's divinity and value are frivolous, for indeed, they serve a valuable purpose. Some need to be reminded more often than others. Be gentle with those whose minds dwell on values of money and stones. They are less fortunate, for they know not the true value of life and of love. Instead, they try to build their value on outer appearances. This is like building a castle of snow in the summer. The soul does not relate to dollar values and will continually seek out more. Be happy with what you have. Know that pride in having more will only bring the fear of losing it all. Build your castle with a love for life, and the castle will stand for all of eternity. Be kind to those who do not understand these principles, for they need your kindness more than anything. They seek grace through a hardened rock. Remind them that they are loved. That is the reason for their display, to feel loved. Bless them, for indeed they are in need of your blessing. And, Bless you, for being generous with those less fortunate than yourself. MARY

*M*ale/Female Energies

QUESTION: Are there differences between men and women?

ANSWER: Yes, of course. The reason that it is necessary for differences between men and women is so that each can manifest on the physical plane. In spiritual form, there is no sex difference. There is no distinction save for differences in your energies. However, when something is made manifest on the physical plane, there needs to be an equal and distinct opposite creation in order to have energetic balance. Look at mankind as the result of change in energy forms. As spirit, you are in a less dense energy form, then you create a denser physical body. For each creation of the physical, there must be an equal and opposite reaction. At your creation, there was a split of energy: that which formed the female counterpart, and that which formed the male counterpart. That is what is meant by "Twin Flames." A twin flame is an opposite of yours in many ways. He/she is also your counterpart in other areas of your lives, though his or her energy will be very much the same in quality. You could walk right past your twin flame without recognizing him or her because of the similarity in your energies. This is not to say that you would not be happy with your twin flame. Quite the contrary. There are many challenges there, but many rewards as well.

Sometimes one will be born into the sex that is opposite to the energy that they are most comfortable with. Remember I said that in spirit there is no distinction of sexes. If a spirit is more sympathetic with the female energy, and is born a male, this can produce the experience of same sex preference and imitations. Inside, the person will swear that he is a woman. Outside, they have the appearance of a man. This is not always the case, but sometimes. MARY

*P*MS

QUESTION: I have such a terrible time when I am premenstrual. I hate myself at these times and want to know what I can do about it.

ANSWER: Dear Child, this is a common experience for women in your times. There are certain aspects of this phenomenon which are physical in nature, relating to your hormones and physical changes. These changes can be eased with vitamin therapy and herbs. There is much written material on this subject. What I am concerned with, however, is the approach to the psychological and spiritual aspects of premenstrual stress syndrome.

Psychologically, PMS has its roots as far back as your birth, though it causes you discomfort in your adult years. Infants have the ability to pick up many forms of information and communication, whether they be through verbal channels or through the reading of another's mind. In your particular case, your father was disappointed with the fact that your mother did not present him with a son. In his speech and in his thoughts, he put out the message that he would prefer it if you were not a female. As a result, when you feel the signals that you are approaching your menstrual cycle, you begin to feel the pain associated with disappointing your father. It was not all right for you to be a girl, so, you act this out through rejecting your natural female cycle. Granted, there are some physical symptoms associated with the period, but not anything which would relate to the mental anguish that you experience. How can the mind of a child make up for the disappointment of the father? In the mind of the little girl, the decision is made to reject femininity.

In addition to your father's concept of women, you also had to deal with your mother's example. She was not strong as a human being and let your father have all of the power in the household. He made the decisions, and if your mother were to make a decision herself, your father would find a way to overrule her. What do you think this must have taught you? You saw that it was not a pleasure to be a woman and that you would sooner or later be defeated. You must undo these messages in order to reclaim your power. It is the menstrual cycle which symbolizes your power, that of being co-creator with God and man to bring forth new life. Do not allow for this potential power to be thwarted by others, even if those others are your parents. You owe it to yourself to embrace your power and your womanhood. It is a gift of the creator that you are a woman, remember this. There is no greater gift than the gift of life. As a participant in this gift, both as giver and receiver, you have the responsibility to appreciate life, to cherish life, and to embrace life. Attitude is gratitude. Work on these things that I have spoken of. Take time to reflect on what you can be grateful for as a woman. You will see. A change in attitude will bring you a greater gift than you now have. Bless you. Indeed, as a woman, you are a blessing to all of life and all of mankind. MARY

World Predictions

QUESTION: I have read many different predictions about earth changes in which Los Angeles would fall into the sea and New York City would be destroyed in a hurricane. Are these predictions true?

ANSWER: Dear Child, these predictions of which you speak have come out of the mouths of many different prophets. I will not deny that this is what they did see and this is what they were told, for indeed there is every possibility that they did see these events as they were presented to you. However, there are certain things that come from the mouths of spirit which need to be looked at in a different way. I know from experience that the physical plane can be very deceptive, even tricky. It leaves you in the position that you would only believe that which you could touch or experience with your senses. When a prophet is talking with a spiritual being, that spiritual being has a different perception altogether. Perhaps it would help for you to look at their messages in terms of what they mean in spiritual or symbolic terms.

Water symbolizes emotional or spiritual energy. Los Angeles, the city of Angels, has been predicted to fall into the sea of spirituality. Has this not already happened to a certain degree? Have not the peoples of Los Angeles in many ways taken the lead in terms of exploring different spiritual practices? Realize that the City of Angels did not get its name by accident. There is a great blessing which protects the city. In addition to the spiritual activity there, there is also a great degree of instability due to the shifts in the land formations. There is nearby Lemuria, constantly pushing upwards against its watery burial. There will be much physical activity in the area of Los Angeles, Hawaii, Japan, all of the land which surrounds Lemuria. Los Angeles need not go into the physical sea. The area is trying to re-balance itself through shifting and movement. Follow the lead of this area, and seek to re-balance your lives spiritually. This will help correct the situation.

Regarding a message that New York would be ruined in a hurricane: New York in many ways is the center of commerce in the world. Most major banks, international politics, and commercial interests reside in New York City. The wind, representing the mind or thought forms, would then be the ruin of this city. Take warning that it is indeed thought forms which would easily destroy this city and the industry therein. There is much fear in this city, and for that reason, it will attract the wind, or better put, thoughts propelled by emotion. The fearful thoughts which come as the result of living in a condition of fear are all that is necessary to ruin a city. If enough people are afraid, it will attract something to fear in the physical so as to have their fears brought to reality in a physical form. For you to look at your own fears and become a master of them would help yourself and others.

I will not say whether or not either of these things will take place, for it more relies on attitudes towards change. Two very different cities with two very different attitudes. Los Angeles, with the constant threat of destruction over its head, has a population relatively low in fear. New York, with no real earthly threats has found a way to create fear anyway. Look at the history of these cities themselves to know the reasons for the differences. The plight of Los Angeles and of New York City are symbolic of the plight of all of mankind. Look inward to find the solution. See in what ways you create fear for yourself, making it difficult for you to accept change. Trust in yourself that no matter what, you can find a way to handle any situation. Have faith that your Creator has the wisdom not to give you a blow that you could not handle. Let go of fear, retain your instincts. Move when the instincts dictate, notice only when fears object. Look at the fears and simply say, "That is what fear looks like." Fear needs no more acknowledgment than that. Allow for your own inner wisdom and courage to come forth. Rely not on prophets, for their interpretations may be far different from yours. Interpret for yourself, for it is you who must take all actions in your own life. Bless you, for I know that you will find your inner voice and heed it. MARY

QUESTION: Is there anything that you can explain regarding East Europe and the changes taking place there?

ANSWER: All activity there is symbolic of the changes in mankind. There has come a time in which man must realize his self dominion, his power, and his part in co-creation. Many who have been living under the rule of those leaders who would take away a man's personal will, are finding release of spirit through freedom in politics. Likewise, men and women everywhere are attempting to free themselves from prisons of every kind: physical, emotional, and mental imprisonment. This does not mean that these people necessarily know what to do with this freedom. People who have not been self governing for some time tend to go through a phase of learning to be responsible with their new found power. Look at the history books for examples of newly freed peoples who took next to no time at all to recreate oppression for themselves. A country also needs time to discover the differences between power and oppression. Mankind must look to itself and in a united front, throw off oppression of all kinds. If you are held back by a past that was unfortunate, you are oppressing yourself with memory and fear. It is just as important for you to examine yourself as it will be for the governments of these countries to do so. For, all of mankind must be healed, not just some. A victory of freedom for any of your brothers is a victory of freedom for you. Look at the ways in which you govern yourself, as these countries are doing. Bring out the culprit of fear that so cruelly oppresses you. Claim your own freedom. You are intrinsically connected to brothers and sisters all around the world. Be concerned for all of mankind, for they truly are your brothers. Be concerned with yourselves also, for your growth will help to free others. Bless you, for ultimately you will find freedom: emotionally, financially, mentally, and physically. I am available to assist you in these matters. I AM MARY

*A*rchangel Chamuel on Love and Life

QUESTION: I am confused. How do I know what is the right thing for me to do? Why am I here?

ANSWER: Dear Child, this physical life that you now participate in can be terribly confusing. The reason for the confusion is because you have so many different kinds of input, and your mind is trying to make some order of your life. At times, these inputs conflict with each other: the heart disagrees with the head, or the physical disagrees with the mental. When there is conflict within the mind and emotions, confusion is the result. The mind would like a road map that points out the direction with some reliability. Because your future depends on your thoughts, beliefs, and actions, it is often unsure. This is the cause of your distress.

In order to change the pattern, you need to formulate a system for creating balance in your life. Notice that you have four distinct parts of yourself; You have a Physical Body to move you about and provide a pleasurable "house" for you to live in; Feelings, which connect you with fellow creatures; Thoughts, which formulate the basis for action or movement; and a Spirit, which feeds you life-force and energy. Each part serves its purpose and you experience each differently. When the different parts are in conflict, you experience anxiety. For instance, if your mind were instructing the body to stand up, and the body actually fell down, you would need to recover the mind from its expectations and begin the process over again. Likewise, if you were to marry one who you did not love because your mind thought it would be a good idea, eventually the emotions would revolt, causing problems in your marriage. Two parts cannot work effectively while they are in conflict with each other. They work best when they are in agreement.

What you need to do is begin to look at the places in your life that do not agree. There are those who are unsure what part of themselves is in control. The person who would marry according to the wishes of the mind is allowing the emotional life to be run by the rational mind. Emotion is a part of life, one fourth of it, and should not be cast away so lightly. If you could take a look at and make some changes in how you approach the different areas of your life, you would begin to create a balance for yourself. In addition, if one part of the being is ignored, such as the emotional body in our example, it then has a difficult time assisting the other parts when they need help. If you have not allowed yourself to feel your emotions, you have told yourself that you refuse to feel. When it comes time for you to assist your life through your feelings, perhaps through love or happiness, you find that you no longer have access to the emotions at all. This loss of love and happiness then begins to affect your physical, making you feel lethargic, or even sick. This is the basis for many illnesses. Your physicians have learned how to affect the physical body but have barely scratched the surface of the causes of many diseases. The advantage in this phenomenon, the interchange of the four bodies, is that you can heal one part through the stimulation of healing power in another part. For instance, you can heal the emotions through changing how the mind thinks. Or, you can heal the body by simply allowing the emotions to be expressed. There are many avenues open to you to heal yourself. New understandings and new kinds of healing are developed every day. There is a great deal of self-help literature that you can read, workshops that you can take, therapies, and schools. There is more information and understanding available now than at any time in man's history. You have read or heard about times past during great civilizations of Lemuria or Atlantis, that they were advanced in technology, healing, and communications. This is true. However, you have even more assistance now than was available then. In these times, you have available to you the accumulation of all the good that ever existed being brought forth into your present. Past healings have accumulated to create the most opportune time in history to learn to heal yourself. This is what is referred to as the dawning of the Golden Age. You are alive at a most exciting time, whether you know it or not. Think of how graced you are to be alive at the building of this pinnacle. It is through the life and love and grace of all the individuals alive today that the Golden Age will come about. Look about you. Are these not exciting times? You, my dear friend, are here to be a very special part of the ushering in of the Golden Age. In the process, you will learn things about yourself that will amaze you. One of the ways that you will help usher in the Golden Age is to heal yourself, allow others to heal you, and help others to be healed. If you can begin to focus on these three things, you will find great meaning in your life. How you do this is totally up to you. Your healing may be covert in nature, or it may be a part of your work. Learn to love yourself and others enough to be a healing influence wherever you go. Bless you, for if you would call upon me at any time, I will infuse the flame of love in your heart and assist in your healing. Bless You. I AM CHAMUEL

QUESTION: What is my spiritual path?

ANSWER: There are actually two questions that you are asking. One is how to know what your spiritual path is, and the other is how to express this in your every day life. I, who am totally of spirit, also must know my path and express it in some way. I am at all times expressing my energy to all of life as guardian over love and feelings. This is how I express my spiritual path. I came to this knowing of my spiritual path through eons of experience. Your discovery of your spiritual path shall be handed to you. It will reveal itself through your experiences, your feelings, your thoughts, and your fascinations. Those things that you love and are drawn to are what attract you to your spiritual path. How you express your spirit is based upon your decisions and actions in this lifetime. Man does indeed have free will. You are not destined to do this or that. There are many choices that you will make which speed up or delay your arrival at eternal grace. Sooner or later, you will get there. There is no rush. Along the way, you are learning, growing, gaining understanding of yourself and others, collecting love and grace.

It is important that your free will be exercised in discovering your purpose as it allows you to create what you WANT in your life. As you live your life, you are gaining in mastery and in power, all the while making it easier and easier for you to create what you love. I do warn you now that if you are in a life in which you are not doing what you want, you need to pull the plug on some of your creations. Find ways that you can improve the situations in your life so that all expressions of your life are reflections of who you truly are. The expression, "Cleanliness is next to Godliness" has always interested me. Cleanliness is the reflection of one who has clarity in life. All trash is the physical manifestation of misused energy. How much energy do you misuse? People must begin to look at their lives in terms of consumption. How much energy is available to you? Infinite amounts. However, as you know, energy cannot be created or destroyed. It can only change form. So, if you are given life through the Creator and you use it to store old fears and disappointments, they will become your experiences. These experiences will weigh you down and prevent you from having new, more fulfilling creations. If you are interested in making your dreams come true, get rid of the trash in your life. Get rid of all thoughts which interfere with your ability to co-create with God. Let go of the emotions which stop you from living life to the fullest. Be mindful of your use of the physical things around you. Simplify. It is through love for life and respect for life that your spiritual path will unfold. Be patient with yourself. You already walk upon your own spiritual path. What other path could you possibly be on? When you clear your life of those things that don't work well, you begin to see a way to express your spirituality on the earth. This will happen for you. Bless you. You and I are forever related. If you

would like assistance in revealing your love and spiritual nature, I would be glad to be of help. Please call upon me.
I AM CHAMUEL

QUESTION: Is there any way that I can shortcut my path, get to where I want to be any faster?

ANSWER: My Sweet Child, where are you trying to go? Your question leads me to believe that you are making a strong effort to get somewhere else. You are on your spiritual path; you are there. Your life is a clear reflection of where you are on this path. If there is somewhere else that you want to go, why don't you? You are exactly where you have led yourself through a series of decisions and actions. If there is somewhere else that you want to be, then you'll have to make different decisions and take different actions. There is nothing in your life that is out of your control. You have experienced everything for a very special reason. Do not struggle with your problems. Do not try to wrestle them to the ground. Do not try to blow them up. Realize that first and foremost, you have brought these problems into your life so that you can learn something very important. If that lesson is brought to you in the guise of a problem, you will have to learn the lesson to get rid of the problem. Ignore the problem and it does not go away. LOOK AT IT! What have you learned from having this problem? About yourself? About others? Step back without emotion and evaluate carefully every blessing that this problem has brought. You will sooner or later decide that you are tired of having this problem in your life. Once the decision is made, you can calmly and rationally discover ways to alleviate it. In this process, the emotions will be healed as the thinking mind assists. Discover yourself through the calm watching of yourself: your patterns and habits; your thoughts and beliefs. Discover warning signals before bad feelings begin. If something does not feel good to you in your life, there is a reason. Generally, it reflects how you think and feel about yourself. There is no one outside of you causing you to think or act the way you do. That is totally your responsibility. If you want to have peace in your life, create it by being peaceful. There are always opportunities for you to change yourself. When you see some behavior in another which upsets you, look at that behavior in yourself and how hard you try to suppress it. There is always a reason why something upsets you. If you were to see all of life through the eyes of God, you would see that there is no need to be impatient with any form of life, especially yourself. You, too, are part of beloved life, learning, growing, expanding, becoming more and more who you are in Spirit: powerful, blessed, and graced. Be mindful of yourself and responsible for your own circumstances. Bless you, you will achieve balance in this matter. Call upon my Flame of Adoration to blaze within your heart of hearts, that I may better assist you in adoration of all of life, most importantly of yourself. Greatly Beloved, I AM at your service. CHAMUEL

❖

*P*ersonality Disorders

QUESTION: Why do people develop multiple personalities?

ANSWER: Dear Child, it is not an uncommon phenomenon for a person to have more than one personality or even split personalities. Some acknowledge their separate personalities and some have no idea that "another" exists within their being. All personalities are developed for the same reason, which is to find power in a given situation.

The need for one to develop additional personalities is fostered through a person's inability to cope with situations in their life. In the case of child abuse, the child cannot find a justification or the defense for being a victim and needs to shut down mentally while the trauma occurs. There is no rational reason for any abuse and the child feels powerless in the situation. The child then escapes and makes room for another personality who can handle the situation better. A new, stronger personality takes over. Additional personalities are usually developed in times of great stress or trauma. If a child feels that it is in his or her best interest to refrain from fighting a situation, this becomes an acceptable solution. The true or base personality can then totally deny the trauma and leave the replacement to deal with it.

The healing and integration of the personalities can be difficult and take much time. The reason that the personalities are shut away from the conscious mind in the first place is because there is the belief that, at the time of the incident, the child could not emotionally handle the trauma. In the extreme case of abuse, the victim receives the message that he or she is powerless. This is a hard blow to give to one so vulnerable. Only in later years when the person becomes strong enough to handle the truth of the situation and make some sense of it, can the information be brought to the conscious mind. I do caution that support is necessary in these cases; one should explore various personalities with assistance. The perspective of the abuse victim is so damaged that truths are difficult to distinguish, realities are hard to grasp. An objective outside party is helpful in the process.

One interested in integrating multi-personalities must be

willing to face the fact that they had incorrect beliefs about their own power and self worth. It becomes an effort to believe that one does not deserve abuse, that one is truly of value. Do not mistake incorrect thoughts or feeling of low self esteem for the truth. I will tell you now and always that you are indeed valued beyond your own imagining. I am here to help you in this matter. If, at any time, you begin to think that you are not worthy of the very best love and care, please call upon me to surround your being with my grace. If you could but feel a fraction of my love for you, you would know that you are worthy in my eyes and in my heart. Bless you. I AM MARY

*A*rchangel Raphael Speaks on Service to Life

QUESTION: I don't feel that I am doing the work that I was meant to do. It just seems meaningless. Can you help?

ANSWER: Beloved Child, there is not a person alive who feels good about themselves if they are not in service to humanity in some way. There are those, such as yourself, who have taken vows of service to humanity before taking incarnation. You cannot live your life with ease unless you are fulfilling your purpose in this life. You begin to feel restless, as if you are sitting in a seat that does not fit your build. Your work is the way in which you contribute your love onto the planet. If you feel that you are in a position in which your true love is not being reflected, you become anxious, irritable. In order to change this, you must change your belief that you cannot do what you love and still get paid for it. We have said before that money is a form of energy representing love. When your work does not accurately reflect your love, the money becomes useless and loses its value to you. Your happiness is determined by the amount of love in your life, not the amount of money. If you want to increase the amount of money in your life, you must increase the amount of love that you experience on a daily basis. That is why career counselors recommend that you do what you love, and the money will follow. Money does follow love.

Part of your problem is in understanding your purpose on this planet. You came here with a great love for your fellow man; to bring the gift of your love onto the planet. I AM Raphael, Archangel and minister of consecration and service. It is I who coach those who consecrate their lives to service. Now, these are lofty words that perhaps you have heard before. It is easy to preach; the challenge is in following through. In order to get in touch with that part of yourself which is concerned with your life's work, it is important that you get in touch with your divine love. It was through this love for humanity that you made the original commitment. Please do make a point EVERY DAY to take time and do something that you love. Surely, all of your time is not taken up in the task of survival. Man has progressed technologically for a purpose, to free himself for the pursuit of pleasure. Make a list of activities that you love. Carry that list around with you all the time. Each time you have spare moments, take out that list and do something. Each time you discover something new that you love to do, add it to the list. By doing things that you love, you are giving yourself the message consciously and subconsciously that you give yourself permission to do what you love. The more that you do this, the faster you will be doing work that you love.

To discover better what it is that you would love to do for work, make a list of how you want your work to make you feel. Does it need to be something in which you feel useful, patient, professional, appreciated, creative? Make a list of the contributions that you would like to make to others. Do you want to nurture others, to help others find solutions to their problems? Take the time to examine your motives. It is always best to give what you want to receive, teach what you need to learn. If you can do that, your own blessing will be magnified. If you need assistance in reaching clarity in your life, please do call upon our Beloved Archangel Chamuel to increase your love for humanity. Then call upon me to bring about the experience of service to life and the Beloved Archangel Gabriel to bring to you your individual calling. I AM Raphael, Master of Devotion to Life.

ADDRESS: Beloved children, it has been a long time since the gates of communication have been so open between the archangels and mankind. Those of us whose life-force is so beneficial to mankind are pleased to be brought this opening. This could not have been done through our efforts alone. In order for us to come through, it is essential that mankind WANT to contact us. It is our honor to help out anyone in their hour of need. At all times, we make ourselves accessible to the seekers of Light.

The time is coming upon this earth in which many changes will allow people to do things that they never dreamt possible. This could be said of any era. Did your grandfather ever believe that there would be miles of highway connecting all cities for the purpose of car travel? Not when he was young, perhaps. Change is inevitable. This time, the changes will bring people to explore their spiritual natures. Many, many will be able to have direct contact with those angelic beings who assist mankind. When Mary conversed with the Beloved Archangel Gabriel, she was setting an example for all of mankind. When Christ called upon the Angelic Hosts in this time of need, they did attend to him. These are examples for you to follow, not impossibilities that only they could do. Please, sweet children of earth, think of us as friends who love and cherish your very life force. Follow the worldly example of the Beloved Mary and commune with the angels in matters of your life's work, your love, your soul, and your mind. We are most available to any who seek our attentions. We do not appear to only a chosen few. You do not need to belong to any church to merit our attentions. The only requirement to receiving love and assistance from the angelic beings is to be a part of all of life. Stop thinking of yourself as different and unworthy. Your life, your happiness, your satisfaction, and your power, are all matters I am interested in. Call upon me, now and always, to help direct you in your divine purpose. You are deeply beloved to me. I AM RAPHAEL

QUESTION: Will there ever be peace?

ANSWER: Indeed, you will in your lifetime live in relative peace. Mankind will realize the futility of fighting. I shudder to think of all the useless killings that took place in the name of God. Do not ever believe that there is a war that is sanctioned by the Father, that there is a war that could ever call itself Holy, for the essence of the Father is peace and love. War, hatred, and judgment are all man-made, or, as I like to call them, "mind-made." The mind has the capacity to conjure up and believe some incredible lies. Where would a man get the idea that he is better than any other? How could this be true? All of life is beloved to the Father. This includes ALL of life. It is man's ignorance that causes him to make judgments about his brother. It is also error to believe that you can live upon the planet, own it, and not be responsible for the survival of this gift. All possessions are yours on loan from the Divine. When you leave this planet, you can not take your precious possessions.

In your lifetime, you will see the beginnings of peace on earth and the rewards that this peace will bring. There were a great many messages that Christ brought to this earth in his lifetime. One of these messages was that of a necessity for peace. It would appear that many have finally gotten the message. That means peace and harmony to all of your brothers, whether they believe in your devotional God or not. There is no one race or religion that has God's love more than any other. No one is more right or wrong than another. No one has exclusive rights to lands, liberties, or prosperity. All are equal in these matters. To love your brother means to love the ones that agree with you and those that don't agree with you. Love them despite their positions. Positions and beliefs are creations of the mind. Love is the flow of the heart. Do not confuse the two. Be grateful for the differences, be tolerant of differences, for they provide you with variety. Surely, the mind can focus on understanding rather than on taking apart life which is already so beautiful. The reason that Christ said to be as a child, was so that you would begin to love without judgment and be at peace with all of your brothers. Make allowances for freedom of individual will and choice. Give up the fantasy that you need to control anyone else. Being the master of one's self is enough of a challenge for most people. When you are the master of yourself, you are responsible for all of your actions, thoughts, feelings and deeds. When you are the master of yourself, you are not afraid to look at what you have done and make necessary corrections. I am not saying necessary punishments, for that is not appropriate. In the past, you believed that in order to correct your mistakes, you had to punish yourself. You have created a penalty system to ensure that mistakes would not be made again. Punishing yourself has nothing to do with being responsible. It is only those who are not responsible that need punishment as they are not willing to make corrections on their own. You, on the other hand, are interested in making corrections in your life and, therefore, need not inflict punishment on yourself. STOP believing that you are not a good enough person. STOP doling out punishments to yourself. STOP thinking in negative terms about your life. These things only make your life miserable.

Pray for peace to enter your own life, peace in being yourself, peace with any mistakes that you have ever made, peace with your fellow man and any mistakes that he may have made. Those mistakes weigh you down and prevent you from flying to your greatest heights. Bless you, I AM RAPHAEL

*F*allen Ministers

QUESTION: Why have ministries fallen, heads of ministries convicted of crimes? What are we supposed to learn from this?

ANSWER: These are indeed difficult times for those who purport to give others the answers in life. You have watched some very powerful religious leaders be brought to their knees. There are many reasons for this and many things to look at.

First of all, man is more and more held responsible for his own spiritual life. He must begin to look inwards for his own answers rather than trying to get them out of a book. The human mind would like guarantees. It would like to see things written so that they can be believed, proven in a laboratory so that they have some credence. In the New Age, you will find that these approaches are no longer sufficient. Just because somebody told you so doesn't make it right. Just because you read it in a book doesn't make it right. You would like for someone else to tell you that something is right so that you don't have to find out for yourself. Here you have the head of a church spouting every Sunday about what sinners men and women are, all the while, doing those dirty deeds that he criticizes. You could say that a chronic sinner does have the expertise necessary to speak on these matters. However, this is not what the public expects from one who holds himself so mighty. Many feel betrayed by the actions of these ministers. In a way, the disappointment lies in the fault of the ministry as they claim to hold all of the answers. Beware of those who would tell you what to do and how to live your life. How can you be co-creator with God if someone else is interfering in your business? How can you know for yourself unless you make decisions based upon your own experiences. The head of the church of God lies within you. You need not go far to find your own answers.

Another phenomenon you have witnessed is the ministers who try to chase away evil and then fall prey to their adversary. Focus your attention on evil, and you will attract it. Raise your sword for battle and surely, your adversary will make his presence known. You have been told, "Seek and you shall find." Seek to fight evil and you will find plenty of evil to fight. That is what happened to the ministers. When one's attention and focus is on the negative, that is what will come into one's life.

Another warning, dear children. NEVER are God's words fearful. Never does the Father ever want to frighten His own creations. If someone is trying to get you to perform a certain task out of fear, rest assured, something is awry. The Father's words, and energy, and intentions are to bring you to your greatest destiny through love and grace. God does not judge or punish or get impatient. For years, the churches have used fear and guilt to control the masses. These manipulative tactics have not been sanctioned by the Father and never will be. One who preaches holier than thou with fear of retribution has not yet learned to truly love himself or his fellow man. They will learn in their own time. Allow them the opportunity to learn the true nature of any Son or Daughter of God. You need not turn your life over to another for any reason. Your soul is the business of yourself and your Creator. Beloved, if you were to see the love and the adoration that the Father and many of us have for each and every one of you, it would uplift your entire life. Pray for this experience, that we may personally bring God's love to you. Beloved, I AM MARY

The Sacred Heart

QUESTION: What is the sacred heart?

ANSWER: Dear child, the sacred heart is something that is developed over time. It is the ability to hold within one's own heart the image and the faith that others will be healed. If you see a friend having great difficulties, your first reaction is to jump in and try to make things better, to fix them.

The reason that you do this is because you don't believe that all problems will come to a resolution in their own time. You don't have the faith that your friend will come out to the other side of a problem with ease and grace. Dear child, do you not know that all difficulties can be resolved? It matters not what you think your friend should do. It only matters that he or she take whatever actions that they deem possible. You might indeed see a better solution than they do. As you have already found out, if others don't feel that they can implement a certain solution, they won't. To truly help your friends, you will need to have the faith that they will work things out in their own time and in their own way. Your impatience and distress only focus on the problem. If you would acknowledge the wisdom of everyone's soul, you would find that you can rest easy in the knowledge that they will resolve all problems. You need not be in despair at anyone else's predicament. Pray for them, and pray for yourself, that you may hold within your own heart the image of your friend perfectly healed. This is the greatest gift that you can give to another. You have seen pictures of the sacred heart, that I hold and that my son holds. Beloved Buddha also holds the sacred heart as do a great many others. All of mankind has the opportunity to develop this sacred heart if they so desire. The sacred heart comes from the love and good feelings that one has for all of mankind. One must hold the image of each and every individual as healed, as without problem, as happy and graced. Try always to see blessings for others, especially if they cannot see the blessings for themselves. There are no greater friends than those who maintain the faith that all of mankind will be whole and healed. I AM Mary, mother to beloved mankind, and I say to you that I do have the faith that you will find resolution to any problems you may have. If you would pray directly to my sacred heart, you will find peace and resolution. I hold for you the faith and the vision and the love required to sustain you through all of your efforts. Please take advantage of my love and devotion for you. It pleases me greatly to be of service to you in this manner. Dearly beloved to my soul, each and every individual is in my own prayers and in my own heart. MARY

Points of Peace

*A*uras

Dear Ones,

There has been a great deal of confusion about the nature of your spiritual energy fields, that which is known as your aura. This aura is depicted in your art forms as a halo around a being's head. There are those who see auras around people, and many, who try all they may, will never have this experience. Whether you can see it or not, the aura is very active in your life, especially in your relationships. The auric fields are like smoke signals that you send from your body, giving information to those around you, about you and about your life. If you are going through a particularly difficult period, and are angry, this is reflected in your aura which may prevent others from wanting to be around you. This is what could be referred to as your sixth sense: information that you receive about others through auric communications. Your fields wrap around you, at times extending six feet from your body. When you come into contact with another, your auras meet and exchange information. When one is sick or going through rough emotional times, the body's way of healing is to extract negative energy and send it out through the aura. This makes it easier for you to recover and to heal.

It is useful for you to clean your aura in one of many ways. The first is through mental visualization. Don't forget that the aura is part of you and under your mental control. You can make a difference simply by mentally washing away your cares from the aura. Another way is to use purifying incense as has been done for centuries by spiritual masters. Another way is to bathe in floral baths, to clean the skin with cleansing aspects of nature. Another way is to simply walk outdoors near the plants or the ocean. If you take a small amount of time during your day to give mindful energy to the cleaning of your aura, your life will be much easier and your relationships much more rewarding. MARY

Dear Ones,

There is so much confusion and misunderstanding about life on your planet. Some believe that they are forced into life on earth as a punishment. Some see it as a never ending karmic quest towards the ultimate good. Some see it as an accident of nature. With so many beliefs about life, there are bound to be many different ways that life is experienced.

Please know that you did ask to come to this form, that it is not permanent unless you want to make it so, and that you have access to all the other planes as well as your own. Your plane is denser, slower than most. But it is also supposed to be enjoyable, with many opportunities to express yourself in so many ways. Life is that which you make it, that which you do with it, that which you think and feel about it. It will be as difficult as you allow it to be and as enjoyable as you want it to be. Your body and your life are not meant to be a punishment at all. They comprise an opportunity for you to expand your awareness of yourself and your appreciation of yourself and all of life. There is no race to see who gets to a certain plateau first. All are right where they have been headed from the start. So many bemoan that life has been unkind to them, and when opportunities for improvement arise, they find excuses instead of daring to have something better. Thus, they make it appear to all that life is indeed unkind. If you believe that life is unkind, you will continually find ways to prove this belief. That is part of life, to test and revise your belief systems so that you can come to a greater realization of who you are. You are constantly seeking understanding, and your understandings can change as quickly as the wind. What you believe and understand about life now is totally different than what you understood 20 years ago. With each new experience and each new acquaintance, you are filled with new data which needs to be interpreted. All of this data ultimately goes towards helping you understand who you are. Look to others and look specifically at the events in your life and see in what ways these people and events change your beliefs about life and about who you are. Continue to ask questions of yourself, they will lead you to greater and greater understanding of who you are. Your imagination can grow in increments, so don't expect all the answers at once. There is a digestion process that the mind must go through. Be patient with yourself and with your life. All is revealed in time. Believe in your own greatness and your own potential to be fully alive. You will attract this through your beliefs. MARY

Help and Faith

Dear Ones,

So many of you call on me in times of distress and discomfort. Please know that I hear all calls as that is the law. Some become distressed thinking that I cannot do what they are asking of me. In some cases, that is true. There are decidedly things that I cannot interfere in and things in which your energy and your action and intentions are necessary in order to bring about your desired result. There are still other times which your desires will not come about at all. At first you will experience disappointment from not having your expectations realized. But later, you will look back on the sequence of events and realize that all events were timed perfectly and that perhaps what you wanted would not have been such a blessing after all. This is how faith in life is realized and formulated, through knowing that time after time you have received what was perfect for you in the moment.

Often, humans confuse their lives with their fantasies. Your fantasies about your life serve two purposes. First, fantasies help you to move towards realizing your dreams and your goals. Sometimes, however, your fantasies serve another purpose, which is to help you to escape from the reality of your life. One must maintain a balance between one's fantasies and one's reality. In order for the fantasy to serve you, you must take some small action every day to help bring it about. If your efforts and energy are not behind realizing your hopes and dreams, it takes much more effort and energy from us to bring you assistance. Remember this when you make the call. I do not say not to make the call. If you feel particularly stuck and don't know what to do or how to do it, you can call for help with direction and inspiration. Then, every day, ask yourself what you can do to help realize your own dreams. It serves no purpose to lie on a couch and say, "Some day, I'll have the life I want." That may be true, but when your own energy is spent on creating the life you want, it comes much faster. All are here for a special purpose, none with greater advantage than any other. Everyone makes their own opportunities and realizes their own dreams.

Another thing that makes it difficult to receive assistance from spirit is fantasizing the negative, thinking the worst. This form of worry about your life, as the thoughts flit to and fro, back and forth, leaves openings in the energy fields which surround your body. You are then open for receiving all that you have worried about. The more you worry, the more you attract what you are worrying about. Have you not known people who could be so afraid of getting sick that they actually bring diseases on themselves? So, too, your worries attract what you worry about. If you can make no other improvements in your life, try to make this one: Don't fantasize the worst. Or, if you must, try to make the worst so ridiculous that it is laughable. When you make light of a situation mentally and verbally, it often gets lighter in your field and has the opportunity to leave you. Laughter is truly one of the best medicines. People try to improve and understand their lives in spiritual terms, often seeking high and low in earnest desire. This earnest seeking can leave you with a hardened look about yourself, a seriousness which makes an enjoyable life inaccessible. All of your searching will eventually lead you to one thing: a humble appreciation for life. Know the words, "My yoke is easy and my burden is light." Make light of your burdens that they leave your life. Bless you. MARY

Visionaries

Dear Ones,

Life on earth is rapidly changing. The changes that you see now are the result of many, many years of preparation and effort. All revolutionary changes are precipitated by impetus of forward thinking individuals who have a vision and take the steps necessary to manifest that vision. Some visionaries are receptive to the Divine Plan for all of Life which is often ignored by the masses. The artistic revolutionaries, beings who are "ahead of their time," are responsible for planting the seeds of freedom that you now enjoy. It takes courage, dear ones, to come forward to the masses with new ideas, especially if those new ideas place one far from the current thoughts of mankind. Visionaries must be prudent if they expect others to pay attention to them. Many don't proceed prudently. Some die in a state of poverty, emotionally and physically, never fully knowing the extent of their contributions. When you are enjoying the pleasures that you now have, realize that there was at least one very brave person involved in bringing the idea to the minds of the masses in order for the masses to ultimately respond to the thought and make it a reality. Mankind has been struggling for his ultimate God-free state for centuries and centuries. Closer and closer all move toward their ultimate destiny with intention and grace. Give thanks for those who have laid down their lives so that you may have freedom, and for others who bless you in ways that you don't even know. Through prayer, intention, and action, others prepare the way for you to benefit from their ideas. Receive these blessings with an attitude of gratitude, that they may be of the greatest benefit to you. Bless you, I AM Mary.

Questions of Existence

Dear Ones,

Your physical plane is a very complex one. If you were to focus your attention upon just one facet of the physical world and tried to understand it, you would find that with new understanding of a subject, another question is always raised. This is the nature of your reality: that all knowledge leads to questions. You will find that the most learned person cannot possibly answer the question of man's existence. Each person has his or her own answer to the question of existence and can ask no other to define this. In so many ways, not only do you die alone, but also, you must live alone. There can be no other who has the exact understanding of life as you do. Your experiences and thoughts and understandings are exclusively your own. Some may agree or disagree with your perception, but none can tell you what is right for you to believe. This is impossible.

The Buddha was praised for his ability to look inward to find the answers of his existence. Now, all who seek that understanding have the opportunity to go to the Buddha to find enlightenment. However, mankind neglects to see the answers to his own questions, as the search is so much fun to him. The Buddha did sit under the Bodhi tree, alone, silent, without distraction of the physical form to realize the truth of life. Instead of going to the Buddha to find the meaning of your life, do as he did. Sit quietly alone, without the physical distractions which plague your world, and ask yourself what is the meaning of your life. Do as the Buddha did, and you will be rewarded. You have known the answers to your problems all along but have refused to listen to yourself. Instead, you have listened to others outside of you telling you how to live, think and exist. Now, in these times, all will have to go inward, whether they want to or not, to find their own answers. I AM Mary, and I invite you to call upon myself or the Buddha to help you find your own answers to the meaning of your life. There is much to discover and much to learn. If you would call upon us from your heart, we will respond. MARY

*M*aintaining Attitude

Dear Ones,

There is so much for you to be concerned with in your physical plane. It would be helpful for you to remember to establish priorities for those things that you find truly important and allow other things to pass away, like water rolling off of the back of a duck. So many of you get caught up in things that don't really support your goals in life and then wonder why you can't accomplish anything in the space of a day. Day after day, you pay attention to those things that don't help you move forward. One day, you wonder why you didn't place proper importance on those things that you had hoped to accomplish. The greatest amount of energy and attention that is misplaced revolves around paying attention to what others say and do, around what others will think of you if you are to do this or say that. If your attention is constantly focused on one person that doesn't approve of you, you are clearly wasting your time and energy, for that person cannot possibly live your life for you. In the end, you will have to account to yourself and your God, not your neighbor. You must live according to the best standards that you can make for yourself and allow for your neighbors to do the same. Social etiquette is a nice luxury, but when it dictates feelings of guilt or inadequacy in a person, it becomes a weapon of manipulation. Allow others the grace of being able to save face, even during the most difficult circumstances. Accuse others not, for in your accusation, you have caused your life's energy to be sapped by the deeds of another. Do not pay attention to the accusations of others who make you think less of yourself, for they are not the voice of God. Walk gently, Sweet Children, upon the gardens that others have built, that they may walk gently upon yours. Bless you, I AM Mary.

Nature and Purpose of Emotions

Dear Ones,

So many of you search to understand the nature of your emotions. Have you ever considered their purpose? Why would you be placed upon this planet with a certain set of emotions available to you? The answer is twofold: you have emotions to support your beliefs and intensify your learning. The emotions that so many cling to as important in their lives, are actually reactionary attempts to justify beliefs. If you believe that someone is trying to harm you, you will probably get angry in order to justify your belief of impending doom. The anger will spur you to take action. Now, this anger can be a very powerful and useful tool. However, if you act from the feelings of anger, you will probably act harshly and never resolve the situation. It is more important when you're angry to recognize that you are in an altered state of emotion and give yourself the luxury of calming down before you take any action. You may speed up the process of having the emotion leave by simply expressing it in some form. If angry, you can yell and scream about your anger; if sad, you may cry and moan. This will give the anger or sadness a physical place to go without causing any harm to yourself or to anyone else. After the anger or sadness is gone, you can reevaluate the situation and take appropriate action according to what you know is right for you. Let not the serpent of emotion dictate your actions, for the actions could well be destructive.

The other approach to correct any actions that may be made through emotion is to change your beliefs. Remember that emotions justify your beliefs. If Christ believed that he was personally being attacked during his trial, the outcome may well have been very different. He chose not to believe that he was under attack and went willingly to a destiny that turned out to be far greater than he or I could imagine. See yourself and others as innocents, for that is the greatest view that you can ever have. With that view, you are aligned with the Creator and can work the works of the Creator. Be sensible about emotion for you have already seen how easily it can make you do things that you later regret. Be gentle with yourself and allow all people their ultimate innocence. Bless you. I AM Mary.

*A*nimal Kingdoms

Dear Ones,

I do count myself as among the privileged beings who have the opportunity to see all of life in its fullest glory. Dear children, if you could but see the grace and feel the lovely blessings that you send forth, you would not doubt your divinity so much.

There is so much good that you do that you are unaware

of. If your attention was focused upon the spiritual planes all the time as mine often is, you would see such a beautiful glow emanating from not only your own being, but from other beings as well. Each and every lifeform has the blueprint of their divine self, that which is referred to on your planes as the aura. Plants, animals, and people have a special blueprint of their divine purpose. Just as your cells do carry the DNA, the blueprint of life, all forms of life carry the blueprint of their spiritual makeup. Each form of life is indeed connected to all other forms, the plants, the animals, and the humans. All have a common ground in which they meet and exchange information and relations. None is an island unto himself, all must relate in some way. Man is beginning to embrace the animal kingdom more and more. In an attempt to prolong survival, there have been those who have found themselves taking the lives of animals for food and clothing. Still others kill for the sport, and others will kill for the economic profit of selling the hides or bones of different species. So many of you question these practices, feeling deeply for the animals. The hunter would defend his actions saying that he is helping the animal by thinning the herds. These things are true. However, in the coming years, you will see more and more of mankind turning to the animal kingdom as a source of love and joy, attempting to have relationships with many species. The beloved dolphin kingdom has learned how to communicate with man to the extent that now man seeks communion and companionship with the dolphins. The whales will be next. Many of your birds live in harmony with man; those dogs and cats that you so sweetly share your homes with do also. These animals who are intelligent enough to commune with man are simply guaranteeing their own survival. Their communication with you grows and improves, and through simple auric channels, communications with each other become more and more gentle. Bless you, dear children, for all of the animals are gifts to you, because they are a part of beloved life. To the best of your ability, treat them as such. You may disagree as to what is the best way to treat these animals, so allow for each to do his best. Bless you, with understanding and grace. I AM MARY

Heart Problems

Dear Ones,

Every one of you desires on some level to be happy and to have a free heart. You have no idea the damage that is caused by a painful heart. Your country is fraught with heart disease and problems with the circulatory system. So many of you have created these problems by ignoring and storing grief and emotional pain. Your heart is the receptacle for divine grace, not a toxic waste dump of sadness and pain. If you are interested in being free from pain, you need to be aware of what pain is. So many of you have refused to even feel pain, thinking that if you ignored the pain, it would go away. Unfortunately, it doesn't work that way. Ignore pain and it will rest within your bosom, waiting for you to be ready to deal with it. Pain is not a magically disappearing form of energy. The very heavy feeling that accompanies pain should give you some indication of the dynamics of pain. It is heavy and difficult to move. It weighs down all that is in its path. If you store this pain, all future joys will be less enjoyable. You will barely be able to feel any joy when weighted down with grief. Why do you think that a recently widowed person does not go right out and find love again? It is because they realize that where grief does live, love cannot reside. Be mindful of your emotions and what you do with them. What you think you are ignoring and defeating is never departed until you experience it. You are not given pain so that you can try to make it vanish. It is there for a purpose which will serve you always. Know, dear children, that which you embrace, embraces back. I AM Mary, devoted to all of mankind. I come to you and request of you: Ask me to bring grace into your heart that it may gently heal your pains.

God's Covenant

Dear Ones,

I would like to ask you to look at the covenant of the rainbow for a moment. It was said that the rainbow would be God's promise to man of His divine love. Now, sweet children, in ancient spiritual instruction, the rainbow was representative of the facets of God, each color representing a particular facet of the Divine Light. Just as there are so many divisions of sound on a musical scale, the rainbow is representative of the divisions of light. Each of those colors is representative of a God virtue. These virtues are all available to man as actions of divine inspiration. For instance, one of the rays of the rainbow could represent devotion. Each individual does have the choice as to the extent of his or her devotion. A particularly devotional person would tend to embody and create (through transformation) more of this particular ray than another person. Likewise, someone else may be specifically adept and interested in healing. That person would be borrowing and using the God virtue of healing and renewed life. You always have the opportunity to reach forth and draw any of the virtues towards yourself. Each person usually chooses the virtues that heal themselves as that is the lacking vibration in their life. Be accepting of the virtues of others, for each is desiring of their own particular healing, in need of a certain ray. Your level of devotion or faith may be totally different from others. There is nothing wrong with you and nothing wrong with them. Each is on his own path. Partake of the covenant of the rainbow in your own way to best heal yourself. Bless you. I AM Mary

Becoming Saints

Dear Friends,

Many of you have spent your life energy praying to those who would be referred to as saints, all the while thinking that saints are "better than you will ever be." This is not necessarily true. So many of you attempt to bring into your life the peace and honesty and justice that rule the energy of the saints. In time, when this energy accumulates and builds into accomplishment, you too will have the opportunity to choose the life of a Saint or a Beloved Master. This achievement involves mastery over yourself as well as dedication of your being. It matters less what you do for work than how you think and feel about your work. All of your work creates a rhythm of your energy. To be sitting on an assembly line with repetitious tasks is no less worthy than to be the head of a corporation. It is those who are working on the assembly line, however, who have more opportunity to turn their work into a rhythmical experience, the same as chanting, or praying in rhythm. There is less stress on the assembly line than in the corporate hot seat. Part of the reason is the repetition of an assembly job. This repetition allows for the mind to travel to more sublime thoughts, creating a world of grace around the individual. Now, if that worker is sitting there thinking unkind thoughts, they will not enjoy the work at all. Repetition removes the task from the individual's mind, allowing him to create for himself the atmosphere and experience he wants. When one dedicates himself to bringing peace into this world, great things do happen. It matters not whether you are sitting on an assembly line or ruling an empire. Each has his or her own individual strengths and weaknesses, all have the ability to bring peace to the world.

Your values, how you prioritize your life, dictate what your devotions are. You have heard before that it is not good to worship money. This is not because money is an evil thing, simply that it should not be the top priority in your life. You still have to live with yourself whether you are rich or poor. Being wealthy creates its own problems which are not often enviable. Man will struggle with himself, rich or poor. Realize that wherever you are and whatever you are, you have all the authority to choose your priorities for yourself and live according to them. All day long, you are given opportunities to choose between one thing and another. Over and over again, you are given the opportunity to express your values. For instance, if you value honesty, you are not likely to try to steal or cheat at any opportunity. You will choose over and over again to value honesty and not even consider stealing. On the other hand, if that is not such a high priority, you may be tempted to see what you can get away with. And, if honesty is not a priority at all, you may steal often. So, you see, even the simplest actions and choices that you make every day reflect your values. More important than whether or not you have money is what your priorities are. These are your dedications to life, your devotions, those things that you place very high upon a pedestal that determine the richness of your life.

Look carefully upon those things that you think are important to you. So many will make a great fuss over lint on the rug and so little fuss over human injustice. Look carefully upon your decisions for they reflect your love.

Beloved Ones, I am Mary who comes to you. My devotion is to all of life. May you be blessed.

Creating Peace

Dear Friends,

Many of you have heard repeated predictions of doom and gloom for mankind's future. Great seers and prophets have made predictions that, quite frankly, no one would like to have come to pass. Why then, would these things happen? You are not here as punishment. You are here as masters of your own destiny. There is not one of you that is not in complete control over your life. If each of you individually values peace, how can there be a war? You must work alone, to attract peace more and more into your own life as your physical contribution to world peace. You must also work together in a joint effort to bring peace to all others. Peace is the absence of conflict. In order to end all conflict, you must begin to resolve your differences. Start small and work on the details of your life. Are you at peace with your work, your relations, your friends, your acquaintances? Wherever you find conflict should be where your efforts are placed. Start with your mind. Are your thoughts peaceful? Are they kind to yourself and to others? Are your thoughts easy to listen to? Or, are you simply working yourself into a frenzy for the excitement of it? Thoughts can be commanded by you to leave and stay away. Negative thoughts are addictive. They simply need to be told that they are no longer wanted in your life and ask for them to be replaced with positive, loving thoughts. You cannot possibly be a victim of your thoughts unless you choose to be. If you are ever troubled by thoughts that don't serve you, command them to leave your home, and your energy fields, and be replaced with calm serene thoughts based upon reality. Through your intention you can direct thoughts to come and go. Please call upon me to bring peace and grace to your mind. I would be most happy to do so. I AM Mary who comes to you, grateful for this opportunity.

Dropping Your Ego

Dear Friends,

There are many of you who are interested in your spiritual path and are willing to pursue what you believe to be right in order to manifest your divine purpose. This is admirable; your interest in spiritual grace is commendable. There are those, however, who would tell you that you must do this or that in order to achieve your divine purpose on the planet through various spiritual disciplines. The reason that these disciplines were invented in the first place was to correct wrong paths which were being pursued in the past. At this time, I would like to address certain instructions that a great many have tried to follow unsuccessfully.

There are those gurus and teachers who would tell you that in order to manifest divinity you must "drop your ego." Many of you have tried unsuccessfully to do this. Perhaps the reason that you have been unsuccessful is because your ego is a part of you which is necessary for your survival. If you were to be ego-less, you would meld into all others. It is the ego which separates one being from another. On earth, this is an important aspect of life. Many of you are too ego-less, those who are the caretakers of the world and give more than they ever receive in return. Thinking that the ego is unnecessary is a fallacy. Those who taught you this practice were perhaps talking about themselves. It does no harm to trim the ego so that it embraces humanity in a loving way. But to totally drop the ego is almost impossible on this plane. Beloved children, perhaps the instructions would be easier followed and with better success if you were to change them to: Let go of the SINS of the ego. The ego needs to perform separation tasks. When your ego assumes the task of judging others or comparing oneself with others, the ego has taken on sin. It is counterproductive to use the ego as a whipping tool for yourself or for others. The sins of the ego include comparing yourself either in a good light or a bad light to others. It is the sin of pride which is being indulged in when you compare or criticize another or yourself. You cannot possibly raise yourself up or raise another up with judgment. This can only be done with love.

Many of you have been raised in the tradition of comparison and know no other way of operating. Your parents compared you to your siblings, relatives, and neighbors in an effort to get a desired response out of you. Now, as an adult, you search for the rightness in your own life and try to make yourself right by making others wrong. If you desire to give up human pride, simply ask to give it up. Be clear that it is your intention. Be your own watchdog. Pray for pridefulness to leave, that God-humility may take its place. You will slip now and again. After all, it is a habit that you identify with. When you catch yourself, you can apologize, either in person or in your own mind. Do not fault yourself for having lived this way for so long. Many of your values were passed along to you from your parents. The decision to value human life is a choice that you can make. It is not something that comes in a calling from on high. Those who receive their calling have already made the decision to value life. You will receive your calling when, with a humble heart, you ask for it. So many of you feel that you have no direction, as if you are bouncing around on a violent ocean, never quite sure of your destination. If you want to live in peace, you must develop a peaceful heart. If you want to live in glory, you must recognize in your life the value of being humble. Pray to give up harmful pride and allow yourself to feel true glory which can only be experienced in vulnerability. The vibrations of the Almighty are so fine that any protection will block them. Your pride is your protection and at the same time your downfall. Do the best you can. If you would like help in this matter, the Beloved Archangel Michael devotedly offers his assistance. Bless you. I AM Mary who comes to you and blesses you always.

Dear Ones,

Many search for what is called a "spiritual practice." Some go from one thing to another, excited at their most recent discovery, only to feel flat and let down after a period of time. You continue the search, all the while determined that you will find some wonderful truth that will bring an answer to your life. Dear ones, these things that excite you initially excite you for a purpose. They get you to look at life in a different way. They totally change your perspective on some issue, freeing you to feel initially better. Do not fault these experiences, for they are important in themselves. There is not just "one thing" that will magically change your life. It will always be many things, new and different, each liberating in its own way. Little by little you are liberated from the chains of bondage that you have accepted in the past. Bit by bit, you realize the true value of your life. This is a spiritual practice, living your life and allowing experiences that you have to free you. There is no one thing in particular that you can do which will cause you to realize your divinity. It is a combination of experiences and thoughts and feelings that join together to form your spiritual practice.

Some believe that if they dedicate most of their time to prayer that the spiritual path will be shorter. This is not necessarily true. Your spiritual development involves all aspects of yourself, not just prayer. Your emotions are also involved. Strive to have your emotions compatible with the Heavenly Father's, for this is a part of your spiritual path. Your thoughts are involved as well. To align your thoughts with the Creator puts all of creation in your hands. Your body and physical mastery also are important in your spiritual path. Pay attention to your own physical reality, for that is surely where your lessons will be learned. Where you are right now is where your spiritual path has led you. See all as through the eyes of God in all areas of your life. This will not happen instantly, rather it is a "practice" and you need only continue responding to all situations in your life with the highest possible thought that you can have in the moment. It is a matter of choosing with each confrontation to embrace love and life and reject struggle and despair. It takes a calm mind, a peaceful heart and loving actions to respond to the highest of your abilities. With each encounter, you are faced with a choice. With each reaction, you learn something new about yourself. This is what growth is, the learning and appreciation one develops for oneself. Bless you. You will see, all will come about to your highest good if you so desire. I AM MARY who comes to you.

Holy Wars

Dear Ones,

What exactly is this which you call a holy war? Holy war is a contradiction in terms. Men have written about the terror and senselessness of war. It is usually those who have actually seen the stark reality of killing another individual that are most appalled. How senseless is the taking of another human life to prove that you are more holy than they are. There is no race greater or more blessed than any other. To take the attitude that beloved life is not a gift is to blaspheme against yourself. You ARE a part of all of life. When you kill another, you have simply devalued your own life. It is not so much that you have committed the sin of murder, but that through not valuing all of life, YOU HAVE NOT VALUED YOURSELF. Others will tell you that you will burn in hell if you commit a sin. I will tell you that the commandments were given so that man would value himself by accepting the gift that his brothers truly are. Embrace each other. See how much you have to teach each other, how much a unified front would offer to ALL of life. Look not upon your brother as an enemy, for indeed, he could be the one who saves YOUR life. Bless you. I AM MARY.

Money and Love

Dear Ones,

Many times, I have been asked to assist children of your earth to improve their financial status. Many ask me to bring them money for various purposes. I would love to be able to help in that way, however, it would be better if you were to learn how to attract what you want. This is not to say that prayer is not helpful, for indeed, it is. But, if you understood the principle involved, you could make it come that much easier and faster.

In order to manifest money, you need to look at your attitudes and beliefs about money. In its simplest form, money is a physical representation of energy exchanged. It is symbolic of how much one appreciates the energy of another. Since the purest energy is the energy of love, exchange of money is the equivalent to the exchange of love. Receiving money is the same as receiving love. These are the attitudes that you need to examine. How do you feel about receiving love? How willing are you to be vulnerable enough to allow another to give to you? Dear Ones, I DO embrace your love for me and allow for it to come or not come without condition or judgment. Be open to receiving love from others. Instead of waiting for the money to come to make you feel loved, begin now to imagine the love that comes to you from others. Open your heart to accept as much love as possible. There are those that you have not even met who have love for you. How could it be otherwise? All of life is connected through love. Be willing to receive that love for your own healing.

You will also need to look at your habits with money and your emotions around money. If you allow your financial situation to control your entire life, then you are living for money. It is those who allow money to ruin their emotional health that cannot see a way out of their situation. If you are of calm mind, you can use the mental facilities to help you, for there is always a way out. There is always a way to improve. It is the law of evolution that mankind always moves to a higher and better understanding.

Stand ready to receive love and to give love. Practice receiving before the money gets to you. This will speed it up.

Every day, take the time to receive the love of others, all others. When you do meet them, you will receive their love to the best of your abilities. MARY

*Y*our Greatest Destiny

Dear Ones,

All men are created equal, one to another. And yet, many think that another race is inferior to theirs and that the two should not mingle. How often this has been a traditional way of doing things, keeping one's race separate and above any other. Dear ones, there is no one race that is better than any other. In God's eyes, all are created equal, in love, in opportunity, and in grace. It is fortunate for the human race that there are those who cannot see race differences. It is your fine country, the New Land, which has placed humanity above race. You have taken in the downtrodden, protected the weak. In so many ways, you are the mother of the world. For some, the strides in humanity appear to take too long. However, you must appreciate the process that is involved. There are great men working day and night to bring about a better destiny for all. Their work must be completely thought out, carefully presented and diligently pursued. You too, can do whatever is in your power to live according to your highest value system. Strive for your greatness from whatever position you are in right now. Everybody has to start somewhere and some have already started. "If only..." is a poor way to approach your greatness. You think that if only you were different that you could be great. If only you had an education, or money, or better eyes, then things would be different. Not so. In order for you to be you, everything about you has to be just the way it is. How could being like someone else possibly help you in your own path? You are perfectly equipped to manifest your greatest destiny. Pray to manifest your most glorious destiny. For each, the destiny will be different. For each, the destiny will be perfect. Do not fault yourself for falling short of an imagined pedestal. Be humble in accepting and appreciating the gifts that the Father has given to you. For, indeed, these are the gifts that you need. Bless you. I AM MARY.

Welcoming Change

Dear Friends,

There are many breakthroughs that you have been alive to witness. In every area of your world, you have seen an acceleration of technological developments, psychological discoveries, and political reforms. In all, the pace of improvements has increased through your lifetime. Those who are open to change, open to possibilities, will find the planet most hospitable in the coming years. These changes will bring vibratory shifts in your fields which must be dealt with. In order to remain calm in the face of any storm, one must calm their mind. Spend as much time as possible NOT worrying about your imagined fears. There are many of you that can work yourselves into quite a frenzy over imagined dangers. Many worry about: What if.... What if things get worse? What if I can't do it? What if they don't like me? These thoughts give your mind no room for dignity. How can you allow imagined disaster to be the food and the product of your mind? Worry is a form of negative thought patterns. You are paying attention to something that is not a reality. I understand that sometimes when things look the worst that it is hard to brush away those worries. Worry was born out of your survival instinct. You do have an instinct to survive, and when it appears as though your survival is in jeopardy, an alarm sounds to the brain to start paying attention to survival. Your brain will respond. You need not bombard it with constant reminders and fantasies. It is kinder to trust your instinct of survival than to short circuit the problem-solving mechanism with needless worry. See the reality and take the steps necessary to change it if necessary. Be good to your brain. Try to leave it room to think about a solution rather than the problem and to see that worry fantasies are just survival fears. Ask to give up those thoughts which do not support your greatest destiny. Pay attention to survival when necessary, and use the rest of your energy to manifest your greatness. In these times of change, your opportunities to achieve are so much greater. Bless you. Accept your own evolution, accept your own process, and most of all, accept who you are, for indeed, that is a blessing to the world and to yourself. I AM MARY.

*M*editation

Dear Friends,

One of the reasons that meditation is so beneficial for you is because it sets up an opportunity for you to feel peace. You have heard from others since you were born how you should live your life. Everyone is so anxious to tell everyone else how they should live. Why? What works for one person doesn't necessarily work for someone else. Each and every person must learn to make peace with their own life. This is not to say that the experiences of others are not of benefit to you. Indeed, they are. A variety of experiences increases your understanding. Try many things that you are attracted to. Learn different techniques of controlling your physical body, your mind, and your emotions. Learn as much as you can about yourself. For, in this process of learning to be peaceful, practice makes perfect. A meditation practice is not meant to only include 15 minutes a day of your life. It is meant to bring more and more peace into your mind so that in your every day life, you have a tool to bring instant peace into the most upsetting of situations. True mastery is the application of inner accomplishments to the outer life.

I see many of you struggling to meet some perfect standard in your meditations. What exactly is meditation? It is the calming of the mind and the emotions to produce a peaceful feeling. This calm comes in different ways for different people. Some of you may not find sitting still a welcome way to calm the mind. You may feel that lying under the stars is more calming. It may bring you peace to feel an expanded connectedness to all of life when gazing at the stars. And, for that moment when you feel connected and the wonderment of being connected, you are experiencing divine enlightenment. You have expanded yourself to include all of life without judgment. And it is when you are without judgment, that you are at peace. Any meditation is acceptable when it expands your consciousness to include all of life. If your attempts to quiet your mind when the body is sitting still end in discomfort, try another way. Do something that you love, something that is fun, and get lost in the activity: walking, singing, dancing, playing. All of life can be experienced as a meditation when one continually reminds oneself to embrace all of life without judgment and embraces the wonderment of life itself in their hearts. Bless you. I AM Mary who comes to you.

*M*aterial Losses

Dear Ones,

It has been brought to my attention that many of you who are trying to be sensitive in spiritual matters find yourself feeling losses in the material world. You then naturally assume that the losses that you experience are an indication that perhaps you are doing something wrong in your spiritual quest. Do not be deceived by apparent losses. That which holds you in bondage must fall away in order to give you the opportunity to manifest your highest good. Dear sweet children, it must be understood that in the beginning of your spiritual quest, you will need to reaffirm this commitment as so many of your vows have been broken, fallen into the wind. This is why it is necessary for you to KNOW very clearly what it is that you want. Not all have come to this world for the same purpose. There are many good reasons to come here, and not all can follow the path that you take. This is why it is important to take care to never force your spiritual beliefs on another. People believe what they need to believe for their own growth. To force your beliefs onto another only makes you responsible in part for their life. This is what karma is, the acceptance of responsibility for what happens in the life of another.

Often, you have prayed for intervention in your affairs. You have asked for one special gift that would assure you that you had God's love. You pray and pray and ask and ask, and instead of getting what it is that you prayed for, you find yourself losing all that you thought was most important. We do know that these losses can be painful. The fact that it hurts to lose these things proves that the entanglements are painful for you. When you pray for love to guide your life, all that you struggle with will go. Realize, Dear Children, that often, in order to comply with certain requests, there is usually a residue of struggle that must be removed before you can have what you want. Be patient, learn all that you can about yourself. For, as the struggles are taken away, you will learn why you struggled with these things. You will get to know yourself much better. Bless you. That which you pray for will come as soon as it possibly can. I AM Mary who comes to you.

Grace

Dear Ones,

So many of you do call upon me in prayer and in times of need. I enjoy your requests as there is so much for me to enjoy when I am with you. I do see all that is hidden through the physical planes, those graces which are stored within your heart of hearts awaiting your enjoyment. This blessed energy of grace is with you at all times, whether you experience it or not. Though you may call upon me in times of distress, I am indeed happy to be in your presence to enjoy your love. This is not to say that I am not concerned with your troubles, I am. I simply take a moment to focus totally upon your greatest possible energy. This is my form of prayer. I acknowledge all of life through the grace that is available to you. As my energy focuses upon your love, the thrust of my intention and prayer is given to you at that moment. I am in contact with your soul, companion to myself, with all the blessings available to both of us. Dear one, as you are a part of Beloved Life itself, you are a part of that which I love, that which I pray for, that which I am in awe of. When you are feeling troubled, I do invite you to call upon me that I may visit with your most glorious self and pray for you. Bless you. I AM Mary who comes to you and enjoys so much your sweet energy.

Spiritual Experiences

Dear Friends,

It fills my heart with joy to be in communion with you. So often, we who are not visible on your plane feel as though we are misunderstood. This is more of an inconvenience for you than anything else. Often, your mind so badly wants to know what is going to happen that you are willing to believe what others tell you about spirit. Dear children, matters of spirit are often misinterpreted by well intentioned individuals. In their excitement of finding a lost part of themselves, they often turn all around them into skeptics. And who could blame them? How can you expect to describe spirit to a mind that has to have constant proof of things that it CAN see? You can take a hundred people and give them the exact same physical experience and EVERY SINGLE ONE WILL HAVE A DIFFERENT PERCEPTION OF THAT EXPERIENCE. The meaning is different, the feelings are different. Just as these people experience the physical plane differently, they will experience the spiritual differently as well. Often you will want to tell someone else how it feels for you to chant or pray or meditate, and you will struggle for the words. Others won't know what you are talking about. When newly finding your spiritual life, you want to talk to others about your discovery. This is all right. Understand, however, the best they can do is listen to you. Their experience is likely to be very different, and they will not have this wonderful experience that you had simply because you told them about it. Part of your lesson in this life is to experience all through your own physical body. Often, it is through physical circumstances and experiences that you find your spiritual path. Be gentle with those who have not yet had the experiences that you have. They need to go to where they are going, all on their own, in their own way.

If you are looking for a way to contact spiritual planes, go to your own heart. Be still, and ask to see your inner heart. It is here that you are connected to all of life. As you begin to calm down and feel your own heart, you will begin to know peace. Pray for peace to enter your heart, for that will strengthen you immeasurably. I AM Mary who comes to you. I do invite you to pray to be embraced by my heart as well.

Growth and the Simple Pleasures

Dear Friends,

So many speak of their "growth" these days. Adults now strive towards emotional and spiritual growth. Unfortunately, in this process, too much attention gets paid to painful experiences being those that help you to grow. While this is true, it is also true that all experiences help you to grow. Getting lost in the contemplation of a flower is equally as helpful to you on your path as struggling to find a job. Both experiences teach you about life. One lesson is simply more strenuous. Do not overlook the simple pleasures and joys when you want to grow. When you focus on struggle, you tend to get downhearted in the process. Try every day to focus on one aspect of life that is not a struggle, but much more a pleasure. You can enjoy this planet that you are on. Bless you. Be at peace. MARY

*M*aking Mistakes

Dear Friends,

   Those of you who are seeking a special calling towards a spiritual experience would do well to know that what you are actually seeking is not one flashing experience which will change your whole life. One who desires a spiritual awakening does so through committing to this desire and daily taking actions which express these sentiments. There will be times in which you are required to surrender, and other times in which you will need to take responsibility and act. Many wonder at the prospects of making a mistake along the way. Know that there are no mistakes which are irretrievable, and nothing that cannot be made right. Instead of wondering about mistakes, take the time to be still and quiet, and try to FEEL your decisions rather than rationalizing them. There will be times in which you THINK something is the best possible solution but at the same time, know that if you were to do the right thing rationally, you would feel shortchanged, or miserable. Honoring your intuition is a matter of getting in touch with your intuition about a particular matter and allowing for the feelings to give you some guidelines. To simply allow your mind to run you around in circles with no possibility of resolution is a poor substitute for clarity. The more you think, the muddier it can get. Allow for your feelings to have some say in what you do. With practice and acknowledgment of your intuition, it improves, allowing you to get faster and more accurate information. If you are about to take an action and are unsure if you should or not, you may ask that your actions be blessed, that they bring the best possible results. Then let go of anxiety over the result. You have made a decision, taken an action, and asked for the action to be blessed. Your actions will be aided through a wisdom more powerful than your own. I AM Mary who comes to you with every encouragement to trust yourself more and more.

Alcohol and Drugs

Dear Friends,

There is much concern over the acts of drinking alcohol and taking drugs. I would like to address this subject. Man has one fault which drives him to these things, and that is impatience. It is the desire to have things right now and to feel good right now that forces one to look for ways to make their lives more acceptable. Sometimes, people see that in order to have their lives the way that they want them, they would have to do too much work to get out of their current struggles. They cannot see how they can improve their lives, so they try to improve how they feel. It is impatience which drives you to give up on the simple acts that make a difference, and turn your attention to the quick results of a drug. The only problem with this approach is that nothing has been done to improve the situations that you are trying to avoid. Instead, a new problem is created. Those who seek solace through drugs and drink are fortunate in one way: they have the desire to live in bliss. It is this bliss which the Buddha would speak of and the peace which I speak of, that is artificially achieved through drugs. Realize, of course, that all you do is of your own free choice. So, if you choose to reach bliss through drugs, you are forfeiting the opportunity to do so naturally. Be kind with those who have not yet discovered peace on their own. Their pain is often insurmountable. They cannot imagine peace any other way.

If you would like to break free from artificial stimulation, Beloved Archangel Michael is available to assist you in this matter. He does ask that you call upon him repeatedly as you need him. His sword of discrimination will be your comfort and companion. He is interested in helping ALL who would have him as their friend. Bless you. I AM MARY

*T*he Winds of Change

Dear Friends,

You have been warned that the winds of change would sweep your world and bring certain destruction to those who will not repent. This warning could be taken another way that I would like for you to consider. The winds of change indeed are already sweeping through your world, and if not destroying parts of the world, are definitely bringing change. Fortunately, these winds are kind. They do give advance warning that change is necessary. It is those who do not take the steps to be in harmony with change that feel they are facing destruction and that the changes are painful. Look about you. Those companies which rule industry are falling apart with the sheer weight of what they have taken on in terms of responsibility. They are finding it difficult to generate a profit with the added burden of their size. Smaller, more humble companies are doing better. Those who previously wielded political power are finding it slipping away from them. This is the change and destruction that was referred to in the warnings. As for repenting, it is a matter of being accepting of God's will and at the same time allowing for changes to take place. You are in the path of a tornado. Root yourself in your faith, lie low and stay out of the path if you can. Even if the tornado passes nearby, you will experience great changes. It is those who do not pay attention to the changes coming that are most likely to be in its path. Be patient. This is a time of great healing and discovery. Those things that previously were acceptable may be swept away in a flash. The world is getting a spiritual shake-up. Be mindful of yourself, that you may do the best you can under whatever circumstances come your way. Know that corrections are being made, and if there are corrections that you need to make for yourself, this is a good time. I AM Mary who comes to you, and I do encourage you to invite grace to enter all aspects of your life so that your changes may be eased and blessed.

Balancing Your Karma

Dear Ones,

Many times, we hear the call for forgiveness for some deed that you have done. You call upon an all forgiving God to forgive you of sins or wrong doings in the past. Do you not know that the Father does not punish or hold past deeds for accounting? Punishment is a man-made invention as is guilt and judgment. Karma, the law of retribution is also man-made. Karma follows you wherever you go as a reminder to act in accordance with Divine will rather than with human pride. Once you have balanced 51% of your karma, you then have the opportunity to rise within the ranks of the Masters to achieve God freedom. So many of you are aiming your goals towards this balance, and a great many will succeed in this lifetime.

Part of the reason that you have incarnated on this planet is because you can do very little towards the balancing of your karma when not in a body. As it is a man-made form of bondage, you must incarnate in order to free yourself of your own bondage. Upon receiving the opportunity to incarnate, so many of you are full of good intentions to change your past and to bring the final balance to your being. Then, when tested through worldly trials, the initial excitement of doing right falls away. Dear children, this world that you take so seriously is your play land. You are supposed to take dominion over the earth. This means that all that is of the earth can be defined by you in whatever way supports your highest goals. When you give over your life's energy to worry about petty matters of the planet, you are short-changing yourself of opportunities to manifest a more divine existence. It is true that you do have to pay attention to the physical plane, for you are physical and need to survive. However, when you get emotional over the shortcomings of others, you create more karma and bondage. Even if others agree with the opinion that they have shortcomings, you still have no right to ever acknowledge it, mentally or verbally. Before you cast stones upon the souls of others, please take time to tend to your own business and your own shortcomings. The greatest fault that you have is judgment. If you would like to correct your karma, you must correct the fault of judgment. Try to see all persons in the highest possible light. Use the compassion in your heart to allow others to make their own mistakes. You cannot prevent them and certainly you cannot correct them. Be as gentle as possible in all of your dealings with others. Even with one who is truly aggravating to you, TRY to find some redeeming feature of this person, and focus your attention directly upon the redemption that you can see. Each time you want to slip back into judgment, find that redeeming feature again and focus on it. Over and over again, this becomes a practice of focusing your attention. Relax, and know that there is nothing that you can do to change anyone else, so it is useless to focus attention on their supposed need to change. They will find their own highest good in their own time. All who would like assistance in this matter are encouraged to call upon me. I AM Mary who comes to you. Please call upon me to help you to see all of life with the eyes of compassion and understanding. Bless you. You will achieve your goals no matter how difficult it seems right now.

Sin and Karma

Dear Friends,

For many years and lifetimes, your holy men have been preaching to you about original sin. You have bought into this story about not being a good person. It was easy for you to believe. Now, more and more, as you begin to understand the teachings of my Beloved Son and others, you begin to realize that this original sin theory is a cruel hoax perpetuated to keep mankind whipping himself into a frenzy of guilt. Dear ones, you are not born into original sin. To believe this is self defeating.

Sin, in its most simple terms, is the act of going against God's will. God's will is love. That which you do that is not of love would be what you could consider sin. It is also that which accumulates lifetimes of karma that need to be washed away. Another mistaken concept that mankind has is that he is born onto this plane to 'work out' his karma, that all actions you have inflicted upon others are to be inflicted upon you. This is not true. Things do not happen to you as retribution. They happen as a way of giving you the opportunity to rise above your past concepts of life, to act at least one step closer to kindness than you had in the past. You are not expected to suffer to balance your karma, you are expected to ACT. Act in the best way that you can possibly imagine in any moment. That is all that is asked of you. Do not fret over past actions, thinking that you SHOULD have known better. Well, you didn't know better. It is that simple, and it does you no good at all to dwell upon and punish yourself for past ignorance. If you would like to begin to improve your karmic path, pray for understanding and compassion. You may not have enough of these virtues to accomplish what you want. As compassion and understanding are God virtues, you are always welcome to pray for them and embrace them into your life. Each encounter which is painful to you is also the opportunity for you to find a better understanding and to display compassion. Dear ones, these virtues do not go unrewarded. The rewards may be instantaneous, or they may take years to accumulate to a point that they help you drop an entire layer of karmic debt. Do not ever believe that good thoughts, words, and deeds are a waste of your energy. If anything, they are your saving grace. They are a way of showing that you are willing to be responsible for your own life in kindness and grace. What do you think brought the Beloved Saints into the arms of the Heavenly Father? It was the choosing over and over again to act with compassion and speak with grace. Do so, and find yourself in their shoes. I AM Mary who comes to you. If you would like my assistance in these matters, please ask. I would be most happy to comply.

Mastering Emotion

Dear Friends,

One of the most important lessons of mankind is to learn

to master his emotions. I know this might sound difficult to some who feel victimized by emotion. It is not necessary to live this way, though.

Your emotions are one way that you learn about yourself. They are like guideposts for you towards self examination. If you were raised in a highly emotional atmosphere, you may have the impression that if you are not being highly emotional that you are not living. This is not true. You may pick and choose what you get emotional about. If you are continually getting into situations in which you are emotionally excited, you are choosing to stay in the world of emotional drama. The whole world is a stage, and you are but an actor strutting about in whatever way that you choose. You were not given certain lines to say and, therefore, need to choose your own. There is no one outside of you that can choose when you will be emotionally upset. Only you can do that. You must stop blaming others for making you feel badly. It is you who is choosing to feel badly each and every time.

Your emotions are a wonderful reflection of your belief system. If you are always getting angry because others 'don't think you are good enough,' it is because you also don't believe that you are good enough. If you firmly in your mind believed that you were good enough, their comments would not elicit an emotional response. Look carefully at those things that make you angry, for they hold the key to what you believe about yourself. Remember, too, that anger is more damaging to the one who is feeling it as it cloaks the feelings of love. When you lose your love, you lose the balance in your life. Next time you feel yourself getting angry about something, ask yourself why. What does this say about how you think about yourself? If you cannot heal the aspect that you see immediately, do not fret. All healing takes place in degrees, layer by layer, over time. This is so that you can have the time to understand and appreciate the healing itself. If you have no appreciation for the healings that you go through, you will simply fall back into old patterns. Take your time, be patient with yourself. If it is your intention to heal your life, it will be healed. Little by little, find better ways to react. Instead of lashing out in anger at the other person, simply say, "That makes me angry." In this way, you are removing the blame for your own feelings from the other person and are finally being responsible for what you are feeling. From this vantage point, you can take steps to heal what is so painful in your own heart. Bless you, for with this simple move, your whole life will change. I AM Mary who comes to you. If you would call upon me, I would be happy to assist you in self understanding, that you may get to the bottom of the beliefs that really pain you.

*F*inding Your Spiritual Truths

Dear Friends,

If your search for spiritual knowledge and understanding continually leaves you with questions, I am suggesting that you take another look at exactly what it is that you want. So many of you would like to have the 'ANSWER.' The answer to what? Whatever happens to be your question in the moment. I have received so many requests to bring the 'truth' to devotees. When I do bring a glimmer of understanding to a devotee, immediately they come forth with another question that needs to be answered. You must understand that when you are doing this, you are playing the game with the wrong tools. You are trying to find spiritual truths that would be understandable to the human brain. If I hand them to you, it means very little, and only confuses you more. Do you not see that the mind can only comprehend spiritual truths through experience? If the mind cannot imagine a certain thing, it has a hard time accepting it. This is why you can listen to someone else preach for years, and never understand until you have an experience which embraces that particular concept. The mind is like a car. You can give it all the gas that you want, but if the wheels are not touching the ground, it won't go anywhere. The mind has nothing to compare to spiritual concepts except physical life. Be patient with your mind, it does have its limitations.

If you are interested in finding spiritual truths, you must be content with experiencing them for yourself. No one else can tell you how you can evaluate the divinity in your life. That is totally your choosing. I will tell you, however, that the fastest way to spiritual truths is to concentrate your attention on your heart, rather than your head. As Divine Energy is based in love, it makes sense that the heart would be the place to look for spiritual truths. These truths are also not necessarily something that you can ever explain to anyone else. You will get there through your own experiences, and so will everybody else. In those moments when you have questions, focus your attention on your heart. Image the mind just slipping down into the physical heart and thinking from there. You will find the most beautiful experiences there, full of love and grace. I AM Mary who comes to you. If you are interested in healing your heart so that you can have these experiences, Beloved Archangel Michael has offered to help mankind to free himself from the pains that he has created. Please call upon him. Thank you for your time.

*R*eceiving Love through the Masters and Saints

Dear Children,

I have brought to you many many words, thoughts, and images. And, yet, there is much more that I could bring you in an effort to help you make the most of the life that you now have. More importantly, I would like to be able to bring to you FEELING, for if you could feel the energy of those that love you, so much greatness could enter your life. Many of you walk around thinking that you are not worthy of the love of my Beloved Son, of Myself or of the Beloved Saints and Masters. This is a great misconception on your part. Indeed you DO deserve the love that we offer to you unconditionally. When you have it in your mind that you don't deserve something, it won't be able to get to you very easily. There are none who are more or less deserving than any others. All are blessed and beloved in our eyes. Those who are willing to reach for the love, receive it much faster. Forget the past. You deserve love simply because you are a part of Beloved Life. You deserve to be appreciated, cared for, loved, and treated with the utmost respect, as does all of life. If you believe that you deserve to be loved, you will receive that much more grace to assist you in all your endeavors. Keep this concept in your mind always, and please do call upon us to bring our love to you.

If you want to receive love from all of life, you will also need to give love to all of life. Sometimes man creates his own problems, figuring that whatever backlash he creates can be tended to tomorrow. If you would follow the example of those who have had true God victory and love all of life, you would not have to deal with problems tomorrow. Release yourself from your body, mind, and emotions, your addiction to problems. Replace these with love for life and wonder at all of life, and tomorrow will be more victorious for you. We would be happy to help you in this process simply by responding to your requests to receive our love and devotion. Just as one may be devoted to me, I am also devoted to all of life with no exceptions. Please call upon me or my Beloved Son, or even call upon Beloved Life to bring more love into your entire being. God grant that you come to a greater sense of greater well being, every day in every way. I AM Mary who comes to you, Beloved Life.

Points of Prayer

❖

QUESTION: What is the purpose of prayer?

Dear One,
  Your prayers are requests for "divine intervention." Through prayer, you are requesting help in matters that you feel are beyond your capabilities to handle. We are always here, ready to help each and every individual who would accept our help. Except in emergencies, we are not allowed to intervene in the matters of one who does not ask for help. Prayer is the practice of contacting beings which you feel are more powerful than you are. In this practice, you begin to touch upon the wonders of love itself and the contemplations of the Heavenly Father. As you were created in essence through the life-force and thought fields of the Father, as you pray, you are calling upon your greatest potential to come forward. Those who dwell upon the magnificent become that magnificence upon which they

dwell. Through your attentions to love, you soften any hardness inside of your heart, thus attracting more love. Prayer is always beneficial if only for those reasons. There will be times in life when some of you will feel overwhelmed by life itself. To retreat into prayer and ask for assistance always speeds resolution. Additionally, ask that our prayers be added to yours that they may increase and multiply any blessings allotted to you. I AM Mary who comes to you, prays for you, and awaits your calls for assistance. Bless you, for indeed you deserve to be blessed.

Beauty and Grace

Dear Ones,

There are those of you who call upon me in times of trouble. I am indeed flattered by your confidence in my abilities to attend to you. I am more than happy to answer the call. It is important for you to realize that part of what creates problems in your life is the extent to which you struggle with life. Those who feel held down by the weight of karmic debt need to realize that there are ways to improve your lot, and the greatest of these is to surrender as much as possible to forms of beauty and grace. Beauty and grace in the physical plane are those things that make you feel good inside: the smile of a baby, the depth of a laugh, the intensity of a melody, the beauty of a flower, the comfort in a hug. When your attention is focused upon those things that make you feel good, you are healing your life. When your attentions are focused upon pain and misery, you are adding to an already heavy burden. If you feel that you cannot lift your attentions away from painful situations, you have available to you the benefits of prayer. Ask for assistance from those who love you to help you to let go of your struggles, to uplift your spirit, and to aid your decisions and actions so that they bring you more blessings. It is those that have the most difficulties in their lives who choose to dwell on problems. They pay attention to misery and attract even more until they reach the point that they grow tired of having these problems in their life. One by one, when the decisions to give up struggle are made, the problems of life begin to fall away. There are those who are very interested in having problems for they believe that their problems make them special. What your problems are really doing is preventing the feelings of love to flow through your entire life. Think what you are shunning, the opportunity to let the greatest good come to you. Watch carefully those things that you struggle with, and see if perhaps you would not rather replace these feeling of struggle with feelings of love. Sometimes you will decide to give up struggle only to find later that your mind is so addicted to having troubles that you are bored without them. Boredom is a wonderful thing. It is a sign to you that you have mastered survival for the moment and that you can participate in higher activities which uplift your spirits. Use boredom as a sign that you would rather be at peace than to be struggling with anything. In those times, find something to do which makes you feel good. You will get used to having good feelings in the place of struggles, and as such, will be able to choose fun over struggle next time the opportunity comes along. Replace your struggles with a creative endeavor and see your entire life change. I AM Mary who comes to you. I, too, walked this earth and well know the concerns with which the mind can attempt to distract you. Every day, take time to reaffirm your desire to receive assistance from us, that we may better assist you in uplifting your mind from the focus of problems to the wonder of creativity. Use the energy that this creativity brings to you, for ultimately, creativity is your personal expression of God's love.

Praying from the Heart

Dear Children,

  There are those who would tell you that you need to pray in this way or that way in order for your prayers to be heard. Truly, this cannot be so. We do communicate in ways which exceed the limitations of the spoken word. Through the intentions of our souls, we communicate with each other through the heart. If you would like your prayers to be heard long after they have been said, say the prayer from your heart and store the prayer there when you are through. It is through the heart that all blessings may be sent and received. See our participation in your life not only with your mind but also with your heart. This is also the reason that you can pray to any being that you love. We are all a part of the same presence. It matters most that you have some form of love and devotion for this Being. Through your feeling of love, your prayers will be propelled. There are no lesser or greater forms of love, and because of that, if your love for your grandmother is greater than your love for one of the saints, this love is never looked down upon or shunned. You are not ever considered ignorant or incorrect when praying through any being that you love. The stronger the love, the greater the response to the prayer. Dear ones, I AM Mary who comes to you to encourage you to pray in any fashion that you can, to or through a being that you truly love. We all respond to the call of love. Bless you, for I too, will respond to these calls.

Developing Faith

Dear ones,

Many of you struggle with the concept of faith and its uses in your every day life. You feel that if you don't have a specified amount of faith that you can't receive spiritual rewards. This is not true. Faith is the result of experiencing repeatedly that life works. Some people simply know that things will work out, and some, who have doubts, must have it proven over time. There is no punishment for your doubts. In a sense, they come with their own lack of rewards. In spiritual matters, you are asking the mind to accept something that it cannot relate to. As a result, perhaps it is best to cultivate faith in the heart rather than in the mind. If your mind cannot accept something, simply leave it alone. Your heart is a much better gauge of truth, for in the heart, one explores all of the mysteries of life. Does the mind ever understand love? No, it cannot. The mind can only rationalize emotion or explain its causes, but, there has not been in your society a good explanation for your feelings. Then, you ask for your mind to accept that there are life forms and power forms that it cannot see. There will be a combination of acceptance and doubt to these concepts. That is the reason that there are religions that literally brainwash their members. Brainwashing is the practice of getting the mind to accept something that it ordinarily wouldn't accept. You do not need to brainwash yourselves, Dear Ones, to be able to pursue a spiritual path, allow your mind to question, for it is simply exercising the muscle of examination and discrimination. These muscles can be your allies. If you are to shut them down forcefully, you will find that your discrimination in real life becomes distorted. Accept that there will be parts of the mind that find the spiritual life a mystery. Let that mystery be acceptable to you. Allow the mind to question and discriminate when it needs to. If you try to shut that down, it will only increase the disbelief. Faith is the ability to accept something despite any questions that you might have.

The object of spiritual faith is to accept God's love despite your objections. You will always think that you are being totally accepting and yet, as you grow, you will find that you are accepting more and more of this love. This year, you will look back and see that last year you accepted love less than you do now. Bit by bit, as you give up your struggles with your life, you will find that your ability to accept yourself and to love yourself increase dramatically. As you love yourself more, you accept God's love more. If one were to force you to exercise your ability to love in an artificial setting such as in a religion without your being able to relate it to your own life, you would learn nothing. Spiritual development happens in conjunction with the experiences in your life, not separate from them. I could tell you now all the truths that you would ever need to know, but they would mean nothing to you. Understanding and faith develop over time, through experiences that you have. Do not fault yourself if your understanding and your faith seem to come slowly. They are meant to, for if you cannot relate to your growth and use it positively in your own life, it would be useless to you. As faith is one of the God-virtues, you may ask in your prayers for an increase in the faith in your life. Faith is the ability to know regardless of the present. For those things that you would like to believe in your life, ask for faith. If you feel that you are unlovable, ask for the faith that you are beloved of the Creator. This in itself will calm you and nourish your soul. Bless you, for I do have faith that you will find your own way in your own time. I AM Mary who comes to you.

Getting to God Without Church

Dear Sweet Children,

In the history of your world, there have been many different religions created. These various established religions usually started with the best of intentions. Later, as groups formulated and the rules and dictates of the religion broke man away from his natural spiritual experience. Realize, dear children, that God is equally available to you while you are smelling a fragrant flower as He is in a church. God has one rule: LOVE. The rest of the rules are man-made to control each other. The reason why you join a religious practice in the first place is because you are questioning your beliefs and need to have a sounding board for these beliefs. If you do not like the belief system of the church that you have chosen, you will find another one which comes closer to your beliefs. In reality, it doesn't matter what church you belong to or even if you belong to one. The Heavenly Father is willing to hold services right within the recesses of your very heart, if you would allow this. Let go of your judgments and prejudices against other religions. Others are simply trying to seek understanding the exact same way that you are. You are all the same in that respect. Each and every one of you holds the same key to your own grace. Others may help you along the way to finding that key, but ultimately, your God-victory is won by you and you alone. This is not to say that you will be abandoned in these times, you will not. However, in order to grow, you will have to repeatedly choose to love. Take time to search your heart every day and to acknowledge the great gift that lies within it, love. Bow to the love in your own heart, that it may multiply and truly grace your life. At each opportunity that you can choose love, do so. I AM Mary who comes to you with my personal devotion to your heart. Bless you, for this love will increase each time you choose it.

Mysteries of the World

Dear Ones,

There are many things about life that the mind cannot perceive. Therefore, in your lifetime, there will be many mysteries that you will enjoy. So many would try to use their mind to explain these mysteries and wander hopelessly through their lives seeking answers that can not be found. If you find yourself in this position and your value of your mind is so high that all else clouds your perception, I do recommend that you begin to take up practices which you are not accustomed to, that you may have experiences you have never had before. The reason for this is because when thought is valued above experience, the mind becomes closed, expecting all experiences to be the same day after day. There is a certain security in sameness and repetition. However, expansion and growth come from changes and the unexpected. A mind that is constantly learning new things through new experiences will be more open, more willing to accept differences. It is not necessary that you take each new experience into your heart and love it. There will be some things which simply do not appeal to you. However, if you are constantly trying to learn, you will develop understanding for your fellow humans. What might look to you as crazy in another is simply a difference of approach. It is those who cannot accept the differences inherent in humans that become close minded and narrow in their vision. If you are to link your life and your vision with the Creator, you must connect yourself and your appreciation to all of life. Prejudice and judgment are the result of lack of understanding. If you cannot experience what another is experiencing, and you still would like to understand them, ask for your heart to find understanding and compassion for your fellow man. It is within the heart that understanding begins, and in the heart is where it must be found. Bless you, dear ones. As you go through your life and would like to understand that which is a mystery to you, please ask for assistance and look for the understanding within your own heart. It will come. This may take time and effort on your part, but, to understand another lifeform is to love them in a concrete way. I AM Mary who comes to you, confident that your acceptance of others will increase with each new experience.

De-programming

Dear Ones,

There are those of you who are concerned with loved ones who have entered into agreements with certain religious organizations and have found that they have changed in a way that is alarming to you. The term which you use for this is "brainwashing." I have explained how this brainwashing takes place. I have seen many futile attempts of those who would try to reverse the brainwashing and most are as damaging as the brainwashing itself. I have explained that brainwashing takes place when the mind is forced to believe something that it otherwise would not believe. This is done using many methods, often through physical manipulations, sleep deprivation and the like. These people are brainwashed and do not even know it. Remember, dear children, that you have also been brainwashed since the day you were born. Those things that your parents told you about life, about yourself, about themselves and about others are things that you have accepted without question. Your attitudes and your beliefs all began as a form of brainwashing. De-programming yourself is accomplished through differences in your experience. For instance, if your parents repeatedly told you that you were stupid, and you then went to school and had many teachers telling you that you were brilliant, you would then need to reevaluate the original brainwashing from your parents. Through your own experiences you begin to form your OWN attitudes and beliefs. Problems do arise when you add one belief onto a conflicting belief. Our example of the smart and stupid belief would create a child who was actually brilliant but would consciously or unconsciously thwart his own efforts at academics in order to satisfy both beliefs. It is important when debriefing yourself to find those beliefs which are in conflict as they are just as damaging as holding negative beliefs about the self. Conflicting beliefs are more devious than simple negativity as they are hidden and confused in nature.

When attempting to help others to debrief themselves and find their true beliefs, the best route is through the heart. Those who would kidnap an already brainwashed individual and try to force-feed them new beliefs on top of the old ones will be unsuccessful. For the sake of survival, an individual can easily go along with your ploy until you are satisfied, but they are not healed. Fighting belief with belief is a fruitless practice. It must be through experience and through love that one changes beliefs. If your approach to an individual is forceful, true healing cannot take place. True healing takes place only in the presence of love, and it is the energy of love that prompts and facilitates healing. If you are in the situation in which you need to assist an individual through their distorted beliefs, make sure that you take ample time for them to experience your love before you even discuss beliefs. They need to feel safe in the knowledge and the presence of love, no matter what their beliefs are. Their mind will then move to understand that in the beginning of their experience, they were valued by the church or organization that brainwashed them because they were willing to accept the beliefs of the group. In your attempts to bring them back to themselves, you must appreciate and value them no matter what their beliefs are. That is practicing love that is a bit higher in vibration than what they have already experienced. They will levitate towards this love, for love is magnetic. Most of all, be patient, and know that through love and through grace, each will find their true path. Bless you. If you are in need of assistance, please do call upon me. I AM Mary who comes to you.

Giving Advice

Dear Ones,

One of the most difficult aspects involved with giving advice is the karmic retribution that is attached. Those who make a habit of telling others how they should live their lives could be setting themselves up for quite a difficult time. Usually this advice giving is done with good intentions and a loving heart. In these instances, the backlash is less. However, when advice is given with a prideful mind, the retribution could be extreme. There is a difference between helping someone by telling them what to do and helping someone by loving them enough to facilitate inner strength to solve their own problems. Take care when giving advice that it be with a loving heart and that this advice points your friend to a more loving situation. If you were to advise a friend to leave her marriage as you have seen her suffer all you can, and she does this because of your suggestion, you then take on the burden of her separation and may find that you have taken on more than you can handle.

   Those of you who will continue helping others and would like a better way to do it can simply concentrate on asking questions of your friend and refusing to suggest what to do or predicting what will happen. Those who even make their living giving predictions of this sort through psychic information know not the burden that they accumulate. Man was not warned about practicing with psychic energy because it is the work of the devil. It is not. He was warned because if used as a way to control or effect the lives of others, the karmic burden to the practitioner becomes great indeed. You will be tested and tempted to give advice to others. However, you must learn that even if you have had enough of your friend's marriage this does not mean that your friend has had enough. Often, in the desperation of feeling like you can't possibly help your friend, you give bad advice. Others may be asking you what they should do. Your reply can be, "What do you feel that you want to do? I can't possibly tell you what to do, because I am not in that situation." This is the truth. It's easy to make the game plan from the comfort of your seat and quite possibly much more difficult to carry it out. If you want to help a friend, the best thing that you can do is make sure that they know that you love them and that you will stand by whatever decision they make, even if you think it is the wrong decision. You might just know what is best for an individual, but it is for them to learn for themselves what actions need to be taken. Their life is not your lesson, it is theirs. Your lesson is to support them with whatever love you can muster, whatever patience you can find, and whatever grace you have available to you. Bless you, dear ones. If you are in need of this love, patience and grace, please do call upon me as I would be happy to help you in this matter. Resist the temptation to be a know-all as all are different and need to experience their own lives the best way that they know how in the moment.

Conquering Fear

Dear Ones,

Fear is the most damaging emotion that you can give in to. Fear is the experience one has when one believes that one's livelihood or security has been threatened. There are times in which this fear is appropriate and times when it is not. If you are faced with the prospect of wrestling a bear ten times your size, fear would be an appropriate emotion. Fear is a self protective device to assist your survival instinct. All instincts need to be respected and not hindered. When it happens that you find yourself afraid of something, there are a few things that you can do. First of all, check to see if your fear is based in reality. Or, is it based on a fantasy that you have about what could happen or even a memory of your past experiences? If the woolly bear is standing directly in front of you or you heard his footsteps just around the corner, you are dealing with a reality situation. In that instance, the fear will push the adrenaline through your body giving you the ability to act more quickly than if you were relaxed. You will be stronger and faster and more agile with this infusion of additional adrenaline. Then you can act in whatever way you see appropriate at the time. If, on the other hand, you are experiencing fear because you might lose your job in six months, you are fearing something that is a fantasy that you have made up. You will still get the rush of adrenaline, which is not necessary at this time, and you will have extra energy that you really don't need. In that case, it is time for you to look at reality and realize that you are inventing this situation simply to get yourself pumped up. An idle mind is very creative, isn't it? Before too long, this mind can have you imagining that you are in the bread line looking for handouts. Dear ones, imagined fear is a form of negative energy when it is created for the purpose of idle excitement. If you are creating fear on a regular basis, perhaps it is time to examine your beliefs about your survival. Fear is a tool for survival. If you are taking out this tool when there is nothing life threatening lurking in the bushes, what is really happening is that you are attaching your beliefs about your survival to outside issues. For instance, if you are afraid of letting a lover get too close to you, there is something in your mind that says that if someone gets close, your survival is threatened. Is this really so? So many of you base your fears around love, believing that if another is to love you, you will lose a valuable part of yourself. The only way to deal with these invented fears is to call upon your natural courage to go forth in your life despite the fear that is there. How many of you have a dream that you would like to realize and do not even attempt to live your dream, because the fear of failure or the fear of ridicule is stopping you? You made up this fear, and since you can do that, you can also make up the courage to go forward despite the fear. And what if you fail? Does that mean that your life is threatened? In most endeavors, it does not. There are many successful people who have failed in their lifetime. Failure simply means that your expectations have not been met, not that there is something wrong with you. It is just that you did not perceive it as it is. Practice dealing with reality, it will improve your chances of realizing your expectations. Create courage just greater than your fears, and go forth towards your dreams. Be realistic in your expectations as to how long it will take, how much work it will require, how much patience you will need. When you go forth to be a pioneer on this planet, you need to cut a bit of brush along the way. Resistance does not mean that you are doing the wrong thing, it means that your efforts need to be consistent and sincere. So many take the short view in their dreams, never realizing that a dream is a personal experience of the soul and that it takes effort to bring forth this dream onto the physical planet. If you believe that you have tried and failed, perhaps you have not tried long enough. Perhaps you did not allow for the time and effort required to come forth from your being. As it is your dream, the efforts must come through you so that your entire being may mold the final product. Another cannot realize your dream. If you were counting on this happening, you will probably be disappointed with the results, for the physical manifestation came through another. This does not mean in any way that you cannot ask for and accept help from others. Indeed you should. Simply know that your time, energy and efforts must be put forth in a realistic manner, for to realize your dream is to bring your heart's desires onto the physical planet. The rewards are great when you realize your life's destiny, despite fears, despite resistance and setbacks, and despite unrealized expectations. I am happy to help you in this matter. Please call upon me to pray for you to realize your greatest destiny. For indeed, despite your fantasies, that is the best that you could possibly do. I AM Mary who comes to you. Bless you, for indeed you deserve to be blessed.

*S*olving Life's Problems

Dear Ones,

So many lament the times that they fail at something or find problems in an area of their lives. All sort of excuses are made for one's problems. Problems are the most talked about thing on this planet. However, so many totally miss the boat when it comes to understanding why they have problems. Your problems are a form of resistance. Problems get you to look at yourself and look at your life and make necessary changes. When you experience the same problems over and over again, sooner or later you begin to learn about this aspect of life, you begin to understand. For instance, if you continue to have the same problems in your relationships, you are being given the opportunity to learn and to understand all that you can about yourself in relation to others. What you should be looking at is how very important this information can be in your life and how you can change your life to alleviate the problem. Instead of praying for your guides to solve your problems for you, pray for insight into the reasons for these problems, pray for assistance in understanding yourself. Deep within your core are beliefs which you have lived with all of your life. These beliefs dictate how you will feel in different circumstances. You may not even know that they are there. Beliefs act as an invisible magnet for likeness and attract sympathetic energies. For instance, if you believe deep in your core that you don't deserve to be loved, you will continually attract relationships which are not loving. Do not blame others for your problems, for problems are a personal form of resistance to help you to change your beliefs. If you believe that you are not good enough to succeed, you will attract a parent who will tell you that you are a failure. This will prompt you to prove this belief wrong and push you towards being successful. Problems can help you in your life if you can take the attitude of learning about yourself and overcoming that which has in the past stopped you. Every action attracts an equal and opposite reaction, and your reaction should always be problem-free. Use the cues of your life to investigate your core beliefs. Ask for help from those that you love and trust. Be willing to allow yourself to have made a mistake in the past, to have believed something that did not support you. It is not an uncommon thing to do. The great thing about beliefs is that once they are uncovered, they can be changed with such ease. Decide to believe the highest, most loving thought that you can about yourself and about life. Perhaps today you believe that you deserve bad treatment from others. Tomorrow you can decide to believe that only sometimes you deserve bad treatment. The next day you don't deserve bad treatment, and the next day you deserve love. Bit by bit, you will raise your beliefs about yourself until you actually believe that you are lovable and deserve to be loved and blessed. Some feel that perhaps if they are to love themselves they will appear arrogant. Arrogance is the act of thinking yourself better than others. Do not force yourself, do not convict yourself, do not punish yourself. Self love is the act of realizing that as a child of God, you deserve to be loved in the same way. This does not make you better or worse than anyone else. All others are going through the same process, believing the highest possible thought that they can in any given moment. Evolution of your species involves your beliefs as well. Know that you can assist your evolution towards a greater sense of greater well being through thinking well of yourself. Your problems will force you to come to this conclusion anyway. Why not shortcut through the problems and get right to your healing and growth? Bless you, I AM Mary who comes to you, offering to assist you in finding the highest possible thought about yourself. Please call upon me to enfold you in my love that you may experience a greater feeling towards yourself than perhaps you have right now. Simply be patient with whatever you need to go through to get to self love.

*R*eceiving Blessings

Dear Ones,

Part of the reason that it is helpful for you to pray to beloved saints is to lift your mind and lift your sights as high as you can for just a moment. Whatever your attentions are focused upon, you will attract into your life. Focus on the mundane, and that is what will come to you. Focus on the extraordinary, and that will be your experience. Realize that we do try to always bring you good times and good feelings, and so often our efforts are thwarted by the recipient. In the hustle and bustle of every day life, quite often you forget to take a relaxing breath and look heavenward for any blessings that are available to you. There are far more blessings available to mankind and far more graces available to mankind than are being claimed. If you are of the belief that you need to fulfill some certain set standard in order to be worthy of blessings, think again. All are equivalent in their deserving of love. No one is greater or lesser than another. And, when you receive a blessing, do remember to take time and give thanks. That which you show gratitude for is that which you will get more of. Remember to ask, to receive, and to give thanks for all the love and blessings that you can have. I AM Mary who comes to you, happy to bring any blessings that you would receive. You are deeply beloved to me.

*P*utting Spiritual into Practice

Dear Friends,

The reason that so many of you have a desire to seek your spiritual connections is because you know on some level that your destiny clearly depends on this. In addition to those things which are physical that you must focus your attentions on, you always find yourself pulled towards that which I would refer to as your questioning life. Spiritual quests begin when you question the reasons for your life and get no concrete answer from the physical plane. Quite often, this quest is set up by feelings of discontent. After performing a task so many times, one begins to wonder why do this? There is a feeling that something is missing, and you begin to search, to make the commitment to your own spiritual life. This search is something that no one else can direct for you, no matter how much you would like for them to. Many will help you along the way. Many will love you along the way. You will learn things about yourself that you never knew. You will grow and evolve through all of your experiences. The best thing that you can do to prepare yourself is to try to learn with as much ease and grace as possible. Many of your spiritual practices are very misunderstood. You believe that if you are to perform this particular ritual or say this particular prayer that you will be magically transformed into a "spiritual person." Actually, these prayers and rituals are designed to simply get your attention onto some form of life that is more full of love than you are. Love is the thrust behind grace and all forms of healing. If you want to get through life with the assistance of grace, this is how to do it. Some people need the rituals and prayers as it breaks their thought patterns from the mundane physical tasks of the world and focuses their attention on love. Then, there will be those of you who have negative associations with certain rituals and prayers. If they carry negative or lower vibrations with them, they will not be able to assist you to focus on love. Those people are better off simply doing whatever gives them the experience of love. If looking at a flower without distractions brings peace and love to your mind, you are achieving the same effect. There is no right way or wrong way to pray as long as you elicit the response of love. Beware the temptation to become self righteous with your spiritual practice. I have seen far too many walk the path of devotion and in their zeal to see others be happy as they are, they fall into the temptation of judgment. "You would be just fine if you were just like me," is the call of the self righteous. This narrow attitude alone can prevent you from realizing the greatest pleasures, for, there is no greater pleasure than to love without judgment. There is no greater peace allowed than that which is achieved through loving without judgment.

Even if you can only achieve this occasionally, do try. To judge another means that you think that you know through your experiences how another should live their life. This is not possible. The best that you can do for one who is struggling is to see them with the eyes of compassion. To have compassion means that you love with wisdom. Wisdom is knowledge that each person is always living the best that they know how in that moment despite their difficulties. Wisdom is the faith that each person will somehow find their own way in their own time. Faith is the strength which propels all towards their highest good. Whether it is your faith in yourself and in life or another's faith in you, either way, this faith will steer and sustain you. To have faith in yourself is to say, "I know that given the circumstances of my life, I AM truly the best person that I can possibly be. All that I have done in the past was the best that I could have done given what I knew then." Faith in and love for oneself is perhaps the greatest gift that you can give yourself. Allow the past to be passed. Embrace your past as it gives you the wisdom that you have today. Allow for others to learn from their own experiences. Maintain your faith that all will come to their greatest good.

I AM Mary who comes to you. I do have faith that you will achieve your greatest destiny in this lifetime. If you do not have this faith for yourself, please do call upon me and ask for my faith to enter into your life. It will strengthen and bless all that you do.

*L*iving Your Most Glorious Destiny

Dear friends,

There seems to be a great deal of misunderstanding about

having goodness in your life. So few take the time to pray to achieve their most glorious destiny. There is the feeling by most that if they were to live their most glorious destiny, then they would have to give up that which they love. How could this possibly be so? How could a glorious destiny strip you from that which makes you feel fulfilled? This idea of sacrifice is an illusion. You think that in order to live in grace, there will be a tremendous sacrifice on the other side. It could appear that way at times, but I assure you that nothing that you truly love can ever be taken away from you. Your fears in this matter are unfounded. They represent a lack of faith in your own spirit to guide you to ever more splendid experiences. Give up your sacrifice fantasies for they serve you not. Allow for the possibility that you will always gain in wisdom, in love, in grace, and in power. The evolution of your entire being is directed towards ever better experiences and will lead the way for you. If you are harboring the belief that life must make you miserable or that you don't deserve to be happy, you will be creating much of your own misery. If you have the attitude of, "Life always gets better and better," you will be assisting your evolution with the power of grace. When it is no longer possible or no longer practical for you to evolve on this plane, you will go to another. Appreciate the special gifts that come your way, no matter how you are feeling. Quite often, beloved saints will bring you love through your plants and your animals. Accept all gestures of love no matter where they come from.

    Bless you. I AM Mary who comes to you to encourage you to accept your spiritual graces without thoughts of sacrifice. They are gifts of love. When you give a gift to another, you do not then expect them to throw away something that they love. We do not either. Bless you, for you deserve to be blessed with a greater sense of greater well being, every day in every way.

Learning Discrimination

Dear friends,

So many times man confuses the concepts of "loving without judgment" and "living without discrimination." To live without judgment means that you don't place upon another the burden of your "should's." So many choose spouses that they know are not supportive of them and then try to change the spouse into someone that they won't need to judge. If you are trying to change someone else, you are not experiencing love without judgment. If you want another to manifest your desires, you are not living without judgment. What you are doing when you are living with someone who does not support you is living without discrimination. For instance, if you meet someone who is having a severe drinking problem, you can certainly love them with the faith that through his or her own experiences, he or she will find their way. This does not mean that you need to choose to live with them. Discrimination is the gift of the mind to choose what is right and what is wrong in one's own life. If you shun your discrimination in favor of a distorted form of love, you are not allowing for yourself to live your most glorious destiny. Realize that you cannot possibly imagine how good your life can be. If your experiences are of misery, how can you imagine joy? Leave some room in your mind and in your life for the possibility to live in peace and walk in grace. Each opening that is left for the Heavenly Father to bring you love will be filled for you. If you find yourself with an empty or even a painful feeling in your heart, ask for the Father to bring love to heal these feelings. All is not as it appears to be. Change is necessary for those who would like to improve their lives. How could it be otherwise? Improvement implies that something is getting better. In order to get better, things need to change. Look carefully at your life and see in what ways you deny yourself the common sense discriminations that could make your life easier. See if you are delaying fixing things that should be fixed and dealt with. Your attachment to the problem is representative of a belief that you have about yourself that is not supportive. To make bad decisions in your life is similar to making bad business decisions. I have seen so many who could make clear and discriminatory choices in their professional lives and make very non-supportive choices in their personal lives. We know that there is nothing wrong with the working mechanisms of their minds as they function quite well in business settings. It has to be a belief that they can't do better that stops them. Look carefully at how you live your life, how you prolong improvements that are possible to make, and how you face changes. All of these can be improved to bring a maximum amount of happiness into your life. I AM Mary who comes to you, offering my faith in your ability to love without judgment and at the same time practice discrimination in your life. Bless you.

Shedding Judgment

Dear Ones,

I have spoken often about judgment and the damages

that it causes. If you would like to alleviate yourself of the habit of judging others, perhaps you should understand the premise behind judging. As you were growing older and developing, it was natural in your society to realize differences and to categorize others in order that you could make a determination of who you were. It was through these comparisons that you were able to establish your own separate identity. Now, your sages are telling you to see yourself as not separate. This goes against your original learning process from childhood. Another situation that comes into play is learning to empathize with others. If you are a very feeling person, there is the possibility that you have gone through your life identifying with others through emotion. You identify with another and then put yourself in their place in order that you can be their friend, empathize with them. So often you have made the mistake of bringing yourself down in order that you can prove what a good friend you are. Time after time when you do this, there is no reward. The next time you find yourself doing this, try instead the tactic of not being an emotional friend and take a different path. Physically, you can remove your friend from the place of unhappiness by getting them out of the house, changing the scenery. Mentally you can be a friend by having logical discussions with them. And, spiritually you can be a friend by seeing your friend in complete victory, seeing their blessings. If, on the other hand, you are more in control of your feelings and still find yourself judging, this is due to the fact that you feel that you must control your emotions and your environment to the point of mentally shunning all that you do not understand or are afraid of. You see a friend doing something that you would think harmful to him. What you are really thinking initially is that you are afraid of yourself getting in that same situation. It is important to realize that what experiences you need will come to you, and those that your friend needs will come to him. There is no need to fear the way that your life moves, for it is ultimately a reflection of your soul's desires. There is nothing that will come to you that will break or destroy you, for the soul is not self destructive in nature or intention. Thinking that you can be in control of this is an illusion. Your judging is a way of trying to keep away from yourself that which you do not want. It is a way of trying to control your environment. To judge is to blow about fantasies which only waste your precious life. Judgment is the fear that you could possibly be in the situation of another. I AM Mary who comes to you, seeing you fully graced.

Being One With The Universe

Dear Ones,

Your contemporary philosophers have so much to say, and so often, get through to very few people. Part of the reason is that many preach to you in such general and broad terms, leaving you with the feeling that in order for you to grow spiritually or even benefit from a spiritual life, you need to accomplish very elusive goals. You are told that in order to manifest divinity in your life that you need to "be one with the universe." Here you are, inside of your body, relatively small in relation with many things, and you can't conceive of how to be one with something so large. And how do you function on the physical planet if you are spending all of your energy being one with the universe? I do know the trials of this, your physical plane, as do a great many Ascended Masters. You must remember that there are those who dedicate their life to spiritual works in earnest with no other interruptions. The Buddha did not have the responsibility of taking care of children, working many hours a week, housing a family. You cannot be the Buddha unless you are taken care of on the physical plane. Life is so different now than it was when even I was incarnate. You must now be more attentive of things that were not a burden 2000 years ago. And conversely, you also have some relief from burdens that did exist before. Because of that, you will need to consider your whole life your spiritual path. It does not begin when you decide to meditate every day. It begins at your birth. If your lot in life is to participate in much physical labor, this is your spiritual path. Those things that you do and thoughts and feelings you have are all a part of your path.

To be one with the universe is a lovely idea, but how do you do that? It all depends on your situation in life and your priorities at any given time. The concept behind this is for you to feel connected to all of life. Life as you now know it, life as you imagine it, and life as you haven't yet experienced it. The way to feel connected to all of life is to be as much as possible around that which you love. If you find love in the smile of an infant, each opportunity you get to see that, take it. Stop and talk to that new mother and her baby, for that is how you feel connected to all of life. If it is alone in prayer that you feel most blessed, do that. In a way, to be connected to all of life is a form of devotion. It is through love of life that one becomes grateful for those things which make him happy. It is through gratitude that devotion to life is developed. This is also a reciprocal situation. If you are having troubles, you can take the opportunity to speed up the process of grace by devotional practices to life. To intentionally find something that you can be grateful for will jump start your good fortune. Instead of thinking about what you would like different in your life, take the time to feel truly grateful for whatever blessings you can find. Look for them if you need to. And if you still can't find any, please do call upon me. I would be more than happy to bring something that will make you feel blessed. I AM Mary who comes to you, grateful for this opportunity to be with you.

Acquiring Virtues

Dear Ones,

So many of you miss opportunities through prayer that are available to you. There are so many Masters and Saints and Angels that are available to you for assistance in your everyday life. We also exist and have chosen some kind of work that pleases us and assists life at the same time. Your life is not that much different from ours in that way. That is why we often tell you to learn to do work that you love, for work never really ends after you pass into another plane. There will always be some form of creativity passing through you at all times.

Masters and Saints are those who have, through the energy of their lives, accumulated strength in one of the virtues of God. My friend, the Beloved St. Francis earned his mastery through humility and devotion. There are certain things that he understands in a special way that are the result of his humility. He is also a wise being because of these experiences. Just as I AM available to you, so too are many wonderful masters. Some of the churches make a practice of speaking with the saints and masters. If you would like to receive some of the blessings that you don't already receive, it is perfectly acceptable for you to ask. Not all of you will know who to ask for and would still like to ask for assistance. The best way to do this is to find whichever virtue is necessary for you to improve your present life and call upon the Master of that virtue. For instance, if you need courage to face something that you fear, call upon Beloved Courage to infuse you with strength. Masters will respond by name or by virtue. Call upon Beloved Patience when necessary, ask for Beloved Victory to grace your life. Call upon Beloved Faith to strengthen your ties to God. All virtues are available to you.

There are many times in which you feel that you should not be calling for help because it would be wrong. This cannot be so. You are deserving of the assistance of all of life to help you to grow in your life. The laws of Heaven are much the same as the laws of nature. The laws of nature are that which in a sense sustain life on planet earth. The laws of Heaven are that which sustain all of life. It is the discussion of these laws which has held the attentions of your scientists and your preachers alike. The scientists cannot seem to agree on many things and neither do your preachers. The reason for this is because, as you might observe through the laws of nature, life is subject to evolution, subject to change. As soon as your scientists think that they have the answer to an important question, other scientists invent better tools for observation and provide the community with a new opportunity to explore life from a whole different angle. Spiritual law is the same. Spiritual evolution is guaranteed so that once you evolve to a certain point, a change takes place to assist you to further evolution. Let the scientists and the preachers issue their proclamations about the "laws." They will always shift and change. Try to discover certain laws by yourself through your own experiences. You will learn and you will evolve. You need not punish yourself or feel victimized by your evolution. Know always that it is leading you to a wonderful understanding and experience. Call upon the Beloved Masters that they may help to bring you Grace, that energy which will ease all changes with love. Bless you. I AM Mary who comes to you in love and in grace.

Miracles Through the Glory of God

Dear Ones,

Perhaps you have heard the phrase: "For the Glory of God" and know not its meaning. Ministers have taught you that the Glory of God is a dedication toward getting others to give themselves over to your religion. Others have thought that they had to sacrifice all worldly goods in order to prove to God that they are worthy. These beliefs have little to do with the subject at hand. As your relationship with God is a highly personal one, it is preferable that you learn of glory in a personal manner. To do things "for the Glory of God" as many revered saints have done is something that anyone can do. The purpose of doing this is to realize within your own life the POWER and GRACE that is born of the Heavenly Father. It is difficult to accomplish this victory through prayer alone, for the Father is a Creator, and part of the power is through creation. It is while you are performing tasks in the physical plane that you are able to actually realize God Power on earth. Many have witnessed or heard about so-called "miracles." Miracles are events which defy the physical plane and give the physical senses an experience that is out of the ordinary. A miracle is the result of one or more humans accessing the power of the Creator and creating for themselves an experience that they desire either consciously or unconsciously. When doing this, true healing takes place as miracles are not restricted by the laws of man. Miracles are limitless in power, imagination, and wisdom. Miracles are Graced. Many of you now live beyond the limits of man and perform miracles every day. Miracles are a daily occurrence, for they are born of love, and many of you try every day to love more.

When you pray for assistance in your life, what you are doing is asking for help in a situation that you struggle with. As long as you are willing to struggle with this situation, you are engaging it into being in your life more. Try as best as you can to give up the struggle. Decide that you are going to surrender and let God fix it rather than trying to fix it yourself. Relax. You cannot perform miracles while struggling. Those struggles are holding you back from a glorious life. Miracles are co-creations between yourself and your Maker. This can mean different things to different people. No matter how you define it, the fact remains the same: Miracles are the Creations of God working through Man. They are not so much something that has been prayed for but something that is a joint effort. It requires of you to surrender at least part of each creation over to the Heavenly Father. It should be a happy medium between asking that God take care of all of your problems and keeping total control. In those issues in which you struggle, you are not willing to give enough over to the Father. Ask to give up all that stands in your way of your Most Glorious Destiny. You will be asking to give up those habits which prevent you from performing miracles in your own life. Place no pressures upon yourself, for this can be a deeply introspective experience. Then, those things which are most important to you, your very purpose in life, may be realized in this way. There is no way to describe how good this will feel to you. You will have your own experience for it will be created by you. I will address this subject further. Bless you, I AM Mary who comes to you.

Dear Ones,

Many of you think of miracles in terms of large events, the parting of a sea or walking on water. What you don't realize is that miracles occur every day in much smaller proportions in the most ordinary of circumstances. Often, ordinary situations are necessary for miracles to occur. With too much fanfare and noise, the energy necessary for the miracle could be confused. One of the most important requirements for the precipitation of miracles is a humble heart. If it is for your own personal glory and recognition that you desire to bring about a miracle healing, you will find yourself thwarted at every move. It is those who are able to perform true healings that openly acknowledge that if it had not been for heavenly assistance, they would not have been able to perform the miracle. Dear Ones, if there is nothing else that you do in this lifetime, to give up human pride is the greatest step that you can take. Know that true power and true healing come from a Divine source. Those of you who are in a healing trade often get anxious about the results of your work. If you are thinking of yourself and how you look to others, you can accomplish very little. Clients can appear to be far from able to receive help, and yet, you are trying to help them. This sets up a very frustrating situation in which the condition that they are in is not acceptable to you. Why else would you be trying so valiantly to heal them? It must be understood at the outset that true healing must come from within. If you are thinking that you can change them or their circumstances, you are wrong. So many have become frustrated in their trade of trying to solve the problems of others. And, yet, if they were to allow others to be who and where they are, much more could be accomplished. From whatever situation a person is in, there is always a way out, no matter how difficult it might appear. Those that give up on themselves only do so because they perceive their problem to be bigger than they are. If you are wanting to help others, first remember that however anyone is right now is the reality of the situation. Judge not, for what might appear to be bad to you could well be their saving grace. You have no way of knowing. Assist them in whatever way you can to help them find power in their life. Always, always, love them. True healing takes place only in the presence of love. To love someone unconditionally and without judgment is like giving them a springboard from which to vault into a greater level of existence. And that, Dear Ones, is how miracles occur.

If you would like to pray for others that they might be assisted, it is best that the purpose of your request be for "The Glory of God." When you touch another, ask for that touch to be for the glory of God. You will find in this practice that in fact, YOU will be a recipient of this power and glory and be able to pass it along to others. It is for your own sake that you ask to do this as there are great rewards in giving up personal glory in exchange for Divine Glory. In personal glory, you are restricting the results of your deeds to your own powers. In Divine Glory, you are giving the whole process over to the Heavenly Father for unlimited results. A simple way to do this is to simply pray, "I give this situation over to the Heavenly Father and ask that the results be for the Glory of God." You may not even know what will happen or how things will happen. As you let go of your struggle with results, you allow for others to be who they are. Understand that there are those that you would like to help heal, and they are not ready yet. Often, a difficult situation will create in a person a great strength which is necessary in their life. If you are to become attached to this person getting out of their situation according to your timetable, you are doing them a great disservice. Pray for them, yes, but give the results over as I have suggested. The rewards for those who do these things reach beyond the physical. One who allows miracles to occur simply for God's purposes will see many more miracles than those who want them for sensationalism. Stay away from that aspect. Ponder always this mystery, for it will open for you greatness that you have not yet dreamed of. Bless you, I AM Mary who comes to you, with my love and my blessings.

*M*anifesting

Dear Ones,

The reason that it is difficult for man to manipulate the physical plane is because if man were to be able to manifest with thought alone as the Heavenly Father does, chaos would reign. So many of you, if you were to actually listen to your thoughts would be amazed at your capacity to go from one subject to another. Preachers issue their proclamations about the "laws," they will always shift and change. Try to discover certain laws by yourself through your own experiences. You will learn and you will evolve. You need not punish yourself or feel victimized by your evolution. Know always that it is leading you to a wonderful understanding and experience. Call upon the Beloved Masters that they may help to bring you Grace, that energy which will ease all changes.

If you were able to manifest instantly, you would have quite a pile at your feet and no idea what to do with your creations. How often do you dwell over and over again upon a problem that you have? Realize, that as a child of God you do have the same power to produce through thought, although this power is simply diluted. This is the reason that we are always warning you to focus your attention on those things that you would like to have happen and not on those things that bother you. Think about problems and you create more. It is that simple. The more control you have over your thoughts, the more control you will have over all of the events in your life.

In order that you may co-create your destiny, you must stop giving power over to inanimate objects. Why things are the way they are in your life is because for some reason, you have wanted them that way. There are those who will lose things every day and then expend great amounts of energy looking for them and even greater amounts of energy getting angry that they are lost. It is one's desire to play out this charade simply to avoid the real business at hand which is using one's own power. If you are spinning your wheels by constantly experiencing unnecessary dramas, ask to give them up. Drama is a form of struggle with the self that is blamed on an inanimate object. There is nothing that happens in your life by accident. You are co-creator in your life, and the Father will accommodate whatever aspirations you have. You can stand there and tell me that you have aspirations to be successful, and in every movement and thought, you are making sure that your energy gets spent elsewhere. Examine the things that bother you, for you have placed them there by either your thoughts, beliefs or actions. None are exempt, none are accidents. I do not at all mean to imply that you are not doing it right. Look to see if perhaps you feel a need for these distractions and are simply carrying them on because they have become habits. Give yourself permission for having needed them in the past, and try to let them go. You will see. Whatever steps you take to make your life as you would like it are assisted by clear thinking and positive reinforcement. The universe will assist your new endeavors and new beliefs. I AM Mary who comes to you and would be most happy to help in this matter if you would call upon me.

Dear Ones,

In the coming decade, there will be opportunity in the lives of many in which their karma, as it is now understood, will begin to balance. Those of you who have spent lifetime after lifetime in the pursuit of greater understanding and greater life-force will come to a point of needing to acknowledge the end of karma and the beginning of pure creativity. Understand that pure creativity is the ability to instantly manifest that which you want in your life. It has been your experience in the past that your manifestations have taken great time and effort due to additional hardships that have been carried forward from the past. Those things that you have clung to out of security which have held you back will be taken away. When you see yourself stripped of that which you believed to be your security, look again. See if there is anything about this security that holds you back. Allow for the past to slide away and always be searching for that which is greater than you have had in the past. This is important, for even though you may mourn the loss of one thing, another greater must take its place, for that is the law of evolution. You are obligated to go forward. In this time of karmic adjustment, there is the opportunity to become greater. However, there are some stipulations which you must know. In time of balancing, it is important that you keep a check on your thoughts, words, and deeds. To lash out at any one or any thing will only pull you backwards, forcing you to delay your greatest destiny. Do not be afraid to approach your destiny, for that is the purpose of your life. Many have worked so hard simply to be born onto this planet, only to stand at the brink of greatness and be overcome with fear. The fear of loss and the fear of the unknown have prevented wonderful experiences for many. Lifetime after lifetime, you are given the opportunity to choose between your greatest destiny and a destiny of obscurity. So often you have chosen the lesser destiny simply because you are afraid to find your true nature. Dear children, your true nature can only be that of good and of grace. All else is simply an illusion. For those of you who are interested in following your greater destiny, watch carefully that you tend to your own evolution. Be not afraid of change, for change is the basis of evolution. To evolve is to improve, remember this. As you feel yourself going through change, recognize this as an opportunity to look for the highest possible thought in every transaction. Do not delay your greatness by lashing out at individuals in word, deed, or thought. If you happen to slip in this matter, simply cancel or ask forgiveness for your actions. In this way, a habit will be developed of always reaching for the greater goal and ignoring seeming losses. This will propel your life to be one in which you can reach true creativity. Bless you. I AM Mary who comes to you and would be happy to help you in matters of your own evolution.

Laws of Creation

Dear Ones,

There has been discussion over the ages about the laws of karma or the laws of cause and effect. Some of the churches have used the concept of suffering for "sins" which transgress the commandments. Most religions have a similar concept with the conclusion that God will punish that which is considered a transgression. Some of this is true and some of it is false. The "Laws" about which so much is spoken do have an effect on your life. There are certain laws or balances which are necessary for the perpetuation of life in its greatest form. You see, in order for mankind, and all of life, to continue to flourish and thrive, all must work towards that end. As life is a derivative of the Creator, all of life must in some way imitate that which the Creator has intended. Create and destroy are two opposing concepts. As you are a creation, it is asked that you follow the lines of creativity and not destroy. Most of the "laws" that have been laid down for humanity derive themselves from this very concept. That which you do which is destructive in word, thought, or deed will eventually be turned back on you as there is no room in life for destruction. Take the example of a parent and a child. A parent leaves a child home alone for the first time only to return and find that the child has destroyed everything that the parent has worked so hard to create. It will be a long time before that parent allows the child to be alone again or have any responsibility around the house. Likewise, humans who are bent upon destruction of their fellow man or the earth itself will not be given the power or the responsibility to be able to create in their own lives. Karma can be considered the prevention of further destruction by the "child" who has been left alone in the presence of God's creations. It is the same for everyone. If you have troubles getting what you want in your life, take care to eliminate all destructive acts, thoughts or deeds so that your ability to create will be restored. Remind yourself to act in accordance with perpetuating life and love rather than with destruction. Changes will come very quickly in your life. I AM Mary who comes to you, happy to assist you in your progress.

Your Spiritual Mission

Dear Ones,

There are those of you who look to the saints and masters whose lives were devoted to the work of spiritual matters. Their examples can make you feel remorse that you are not doing enough in your own life. Dear one, your life needs to be different from the lives of others. It may not be your mission to dedicate your life to the work of God. If you are meant to do this spiritual work, you will know it. There will be no question in your mind. There will be a part of you which only feels alive when performing these works. There are many good reasons to come to this earth, and if you are not performing works that are glorified, do not despair. This does not make you any less valuable, any less special. Where there is good intent, there will always be the hand of grace.

There are those who are living their lives, going along accumulating things they believe will make them happy, and find that they are not happy at all. There is a place in them which feels dead, that is constantly in need. For those of you who feel this way, there are many options available to you. If you can begin to seek for that part of you which feels dead while doing your daily tasks, please do try. Explore those things which interest you, those things which you have always wanted to do. When you come to the closing of your life, you cannot sit back and say, "I wish I had," for then it will be too late. Be not afraid to reach out with a hand of kindness, for in doing so, you will be securing for yourself renewed life and regeneration to those places within yourself that feel dead.

For those of you who do not know what you can do that would make you feel more alive, consider any way that you can to show your love for others, for it is in the loving of others that one finds their true self. This was the reason that Christ gave the directive to love your brother as he has loved you, for in pure love, one finds true joy. God is full of love for you, and when you act from this position of love for others, your life of grace may begin. Bless you, dear ones, if you would like to have the opportunity to express your love for others, please do call upon me, and I will bring you the opportunity. I AM Mary who comes to you, full of love for all of God's children.

❖

United With God

Dear Children,

I hear so many cry out in their pain that God has forgotten them. They believe that for some reason the Heavenly Father loves them less than the rest of the world. Sometimes when in pain, it may feel this way. However, if you are in this position, it would be more prudent in your hour of pain to ask yourself why you have forgotten God. The

Father is the creator of all that is good and all that is love. If you would like to connect yourself to this type of energy, it is through your own efforts that this can be done. There is no special way to connect yourself to the Heavenly Father except to see, feel, and express your desire enough times that it becomes a reality to you. Even if you have never done anything like this, it is your imagination and your dictates which take precedence in your experience. If you believe that God is a great big man with a lovely beard, then that is how it is for you and accept this. If you believe that God is a force like electrical energy, then this is how it is for you. Everyone has different expectations of God. However, many of you forget that He is available to you at all times, and that your connection to Him is your own doing. When you are in His presence, you have a difficult time leaving, it is so soothing and comforting. However, you must remember that you are now in a physical body, and that body forces a separation from the rest of life. In order for you to be connected to any other life-force, you must make the effort to create the feeling. Think about this. Even if you want to have a relationship with another human being, there is a certain amount of effort required on your part. There is communication, conversation, and dedication required on your part to sustain a loving relationship. It is the same when you would like to sustain a relationship with the Father. Next time that you seek to know why the Father has forsaken you, find time to develop that relationship that you so fervently desire. The results will be very enlightening. Bless you, dear ones, those relationships that you are interested in sustaining will bear fruitful results if you take the time and effort that is required.

My Connection to You

Dear Ones,

I have spoken to you all along in this book about things which you perhaps cannot see and of which you have little experience. There are many aspects of life that you have no conscious awareness of, energy forms that cannot reveal themselves to you. So many would like proof that those guides and angels of which I speak actually exist. There has been proof of miracles over the years, of unexplained phenomena which has baffled the scientists. If you want to believe these things, that is your choice. I cannot and neither can any other, prove to you the existence of life beyond your plane. Too often, those who seek proof, seek proof for the wrong reasons. If you seek to prove something for the sake of argument, you will get arguments. If you wish to prove something for the sake of your peace of mind, then you will find peace of mind. Look always to understand those things which are mysteries to you in terms of making yourself a better person or improving your own life. I have seen countless practitioners of various techniques of energy manipulation spend tremendous amounts of energy trying to prove that they are actually doing what they believe they are doing. It does not matter if others believe what you believe, you must take the stand that your beliefs are enough to justify themselves. If you do not act according to your own beliefs, you will find yourself the prisoner of the beliefs of others. There will always be those who disagree with you anyway, so you might as well accept that as a part of life. Each and every individual who is put upon this earth has a different mission, one in which he and he alone can fulfill. Their beliefs, thoughts and ways of perceiving life must be different in order for them to fulfill their different tasks. Be patient with those whose beliefs do not match yours. They need their beliefs to fulfill their mission. And, if their beliefs are preventing them from fulfilling the mission, they will need to change. THEY will need to change, not you. Let it be so. Bless you, for I AM always with you, whether you have the awareness of it or not. I AM Mary who comes to you, inviting you to call upon me in times of need.